Arthur Hallam M. Brice

David Livingstone

His Labours and his Legacy

Arthur Hallam M. Brice

David Livingstone
His Labours and his Legacy

ISBN/EAN: 9783743344891

Manufactured in Europe, USA, Canada, Australia, Japa

Cover: Foto ©ninafisch / pixelio.de

Manufactured and distributed by brebook publishing software (www.brebook.com)

Arthur Hallam M. Brice

David Livingstone

DAVID LIVINGSTONE:

His Labours and his Legacy.

BY

ARTHUR MONTEFIORE, F.R.G.S.,

Author of
"*Henry M. Stanley, the African Explorer,*" *etc.*

THIRD EDITION. THIRTEENTH THOUSAND.

NEW YORK AND CHICAGO.
Fleming H. Revell Company,
PUBLISHERS OF EVANGELICAL LITERATURE.

TYPES OF AFRICAN RACES.

PREFACE.

"By slow prudence to make mild
A rugged people, and through soft degrees
Subdue them to the useful and the good."
                                TENNYSON.

WITHIN the compass of a few pages I have endeavoured to enclose a great life. As a natural consequence, I have only been able to record the main events of David Livingstone's unparalleled career. So much of that career has been, perforce, dismissed with a few words, that I have endeavoured to atone for omissions of fact by throwing as continuously as possible upon my record of Livingstone's life the gleam of his noble character. I have done this in the belief that, if aught is omitted, or set down in outline too rigid to suggest the glow of life, it will be atoned for by the light reflected from his elevated aims, and by the intense warmth of his love for Africa and the African.

PREFACE.

While it has nothing to say which is new to the student of geographical or missionary enterprise in the Dark Continent, this little book may help to tell to a general public, with scant time at its disposal, an "old, old story," which surely can never pall. And, when reading the chapters that deal with the legacy which Livingstone has left the world, every one may feel, if he choose, the pride of possession, and—which is far better —be led to assume the responsibilities of a legatee.

For my information I have gone to the fountain-head, to the writings of David Livingstone himself. But, as I have drawn upon Dr. Blaikie's "Personal Life" of him for some remarks and passages in private letters, which explain his purpose and illustrate his personal piety in no common degree, I desire to acknowledge my indebtedness to that work. For present purposes, however, I have preferred the public labours of Livingstone to his private life, as setting forth that geographical environment in which he toiled for more than thirty years, and along the paths of which he wandered for nearly thirty thousand miles—ay,

> "Thrice ten years,
> Thrice multiplied by superhuman pangs,
> In hungers and thirsts, fevers and cold,
> In coughs, aches, stitches, ulcerous throes and cramps"—

before he passed over the mountains of Urungu, and entered the valley of the shadow of death.

ARTHUR MONTEFIORE.

Bedford Park, W.

CONTENTS.

CHAPTER I.

PREPARATION (1813-40).

The civilization of Africa—Livingstone—His birth—Parentage—The young "hand"—Spinning cotton—Self-education—His natural bent—His ambition—Studying at Glasgow—London Missionary Society—Livingstone in London—A medical missionary 11

CHAPTER II.

EARLY YEARS IN AFRICA (1841-49).

Arrival in Africa—The Moffats—Kuruman and Bechwanaland—Livingstone's first post: Mabotsa—Encounter with a lion—His marriage—His second station: Chonuane—Sechéle—The drought—Removal to Kolobeng—Trouble with the Boers—Daily life and labour—Continued drought—Retreat?—Onward! 20

CONTENTS.

CHAPTER III.

MISSIONARY TRAVELS (1849-54).

          PAGE

Livingstone, a missionary though an explorer—Into the interior—The Kalahari Desert—A startling revelation—River Zouga—Lake Ngami—" Try, try again "—The tse-tse fly—Linyanti and Sebituane—The ZAMBESI—Difficulties—Capetown—A farewell—Return to Zambesi—Linyanti to Loanda . . . 31

CHAPTER IV.

ACROSS AFRICA (1854-56).

Sickness and recovery—Loanda and the Portuguese—The slave trade—A great honour—Angola—Marching eastward—The Coango and the Kasai—Native friends—Livingstone and Sekeletu—The Victoria Falls—Sowing the seed—A healthy region—Following the Zambesi—Quilimane and the Indian Ocean—Thankfulness 47

CHAPTER V.

HOME (1856-58).

A national welcome—Livingstone's first book—Addresses and speeches—In "the Land o' Cakes"—At Windsor—Livingstone's views on Africa—His critics—Commission from the Government—The Consul-Missionary 66

CHAPTER VI.

IN THE ZAMBESI COUNTRY (1858-60).

Return to Africa—On the Zambesi—The Shiré—The pioneer of peace—Discovery of LAKE NYASSA—Livingstone and the Portuguese—Among the Makololo 76

CHAPTER VII.

NYASSALAND (1861-63).

The Universities Mission—Work of the expedition—On the Rovuma—Mackenzie and the missionaries—Troubles—History and collapse of mission—The Lake people—Mrs. Livingstone: her death—The curse of slavery—Recall of expedition—"The beckoning hand" 90

CHAPTER VIII.

INDIA AND ENGLAND (1864-65).

A remarkable voyage—Bombay and England—Missionary or explorer—The honorary consulship—At Hamilton—Livingstone's commission—A long farewell 105

CHAPTER IX.

NILE OR CONGO? (1866-71).

From Zanzibar to Nyassa—Desertion and report of death—The search expedition—To Lake Tanganika—A great loss—Is it the Nile, or Congo?—Moero and Bangweolo—Illness—Ujiji . 114

CHAPTER X.

THE LAST JOURNEY (1872-73).

Manyuema and the Lualaba—Illness—The massacre of Nyangwe—Retreat to Ujiji—"A ruckle of bones"—Stanley to the rescue—Unyanyembe—The march to Bangweolo—Extreme weakness—Nearing the end—Reaches Chitambo's—THE END—Faithful servants—A nation in mourning 126

CONTENTS.

CHAPTER XI.

LIVINGSTONE'S LEGACY.

"The fragrance of his memory"—His personality and its legacy—Missions with geographical enterprise—The suppression of the slave trade—History of missions in Central Africa—The Churches of Scotland—Universities Mission, London Missionary Society, etc. — Geographical enterprise: Stanley, Thomson, Arnot, O'Neill, etc. 141

CHAPTER XII.

LIVINGSTONE'S LEGACY (*continued*).

"The open sore of the world"—The history of the Arab in Africa—Testimony from Wissman, Scott, Drummond, Stanley, Lavigerie—The substitution of legitimate commerce the remedy — Congo Free State, British East Africa Co., African Lakes Co., etc.—The paralyzing influence of the Portuguese—"The prayer of a righteous man" . . . 151

VICTIMS OF THE SLAVE TRADE.

DAVID LIVINGSTONE:

HIS LABOURS AND HIS LEGACY.

CHAPTER I.

PREPARATION.

FOR a century and more the world has witnessed modern civilization grappling, here with Oriental indolence, and there with sheer barbarism, and everywhere grappling with success. In America, Australia, and elsewhere, the Caucasian has achieved prosperity and content where the red man or the black was but a vagrant savage. This end has been acquired by that migration of peoples and introduction of peaceful arts which we call colonization, and which is only secured when the climate renders European labour possible, and when, owing to the character of the aborigines, the resources of the country are undeveloped. On the other hand, in India and the rich dependencies which environ that unique peninsula, where the natives already possessed a certain civilization, and where the climate is tropical, the dominant English have overturned throne after throne of Eastern splendour—splendour too frequently dimmed by Oriental corruption—and at the present time are governing with security and enlightened justice hundreds of millions of dusky Asiatics. And this end has been generally gained by the exercise of that impartial policy and rigid adherence to the duties of power which stamp in no common degree the national character of England, her statesmen, and the great pro-consuls of her empire. Unfettered colonization and just government have successfully grappled with these problems in the past. The problem of the present and future is a greater one still. It is nothing less than the conversion of Africa to civilization; and it may well be doubted whether either of these methods—so successful elsewhere—can prove effectual here.

For Africa is a vast continent, unpierced by bays and gulfs, and throwing out no peninsulas to touch the outer world. Upon the luxuriant table-land of the interior an enormous population dwells—countless tribes whom it is difficult for the adventurous traveller to reach, and still more difficult for the commercial trader or the herald of glad tidings of peace to labour amongst without interruption or failure. Remote from other lands, other climates, other peoples, other manners, the inhabitants are fearful, ignorant, wayward, helpless, and, from what may be called their "continental insularity," too often savagely suspicious and inhospitable.

For a generation and more pioneers have been busily penetrating this Dark Continent; opening up routes by land and water; conciliating powerful chiefs; healing the sick and safeguarding the strong; discovering huge tracts of country of great fertility—sometimes healthful, but more often hurtful to the European; revealing and navigating vast inland seas, and floating down great rivers from the heart of the continent to the oceans on either hand; exhibiting the practical advantages of civilization; and, last, though not least, preaching the

Gospel of brotherly love. From what these pioneers tell us, we are forced to conclude that ignorance and cruelty, cannibalism and slavery, will only be swept away from the long-suffering African by the slow but sure methods of powerful and responsible commerce—such as the further establishment and development of those commercial kingdoms which have already arisen in Africa—and by the prevalence of what must be an ideal unguessed at by the savage: the well-clad, cleanly, decent, active, prosperous, unselfish, and Christian missionary. None has told us this more plainly, and none stands out more clearly from this group of pioneers, than David Livingstone, the subject of this memoir.

As with so many of that assemblage of uncrowned monarchs, who stand head and shoulders above us by right of their achievements or their character, and whose willing subjects are bound to them by ties of admiration and love rather than of loyalty or habit, David Livingstone sprang from a humble race, and personally knew in his youth what it was to go "forth to his work and to his labour until the evening," in order to earn his daily bread. Born on the 19th of March, 1813, at Blantyre, the hum of the busy cotton factory was the most familiar sound of his early years. His father, a small tea-dealer, his mother a hard-working housewife, and neither with any time to educate their merry lad, it is not surprising that David should have reached the age of ten without giving any special sign of future greatness, or affording any reason to his parents for not gaining his living by his hands. And so the boy was put to work in this cotton factory as a "piecer," and began to contribute his share to the support of the family.

A change in one's life not infrequently brings new possibilities and other hopes before us. This daily life of manual labour would seem to have enlarged the horizon of David's outlook, for he has himself recorded that with a portion of his first week's wages he purchased a Latin grammar! This he placed upon the loom; and, as he passed to and fro at his work, he would catch, now a word, and now a sentence from its open page. With learning came the appetite for learning; and every evening, after the factory work was done, the lad would pore over his books till midnight, and even later. Here we see the strength and tenacity of the Scottish character, for he had to be at work in the factory by six o'clock next morning, and he did not leave it before eight o'clock at night. Fourteen hours of labour, with but two intervals for meals, might well have taken all the strength and sapped all the determination of a lad of ten; and it is, indeed, a pleasant reflection that the humane legislation of later years has rendered such a state of things impossible, or at any rate illegal.

As the years rolled by, and the lad became a youth and approached the verge of manhood, this nightly toil of a general self-education became concentrated on works of travel and science, a subject he still further pursued on rare holidays by exploring the country round. The strong religious convictions which his father and mother had ever encouraged were stamped with the hall-mark of sincerity through his own search after truth, and the relentless self-examination to which he subjected himself. There arose before him—never to fade away—the sublime form of Jesus of Nazareth, the Great Physician. No wonder is it that David Livingstone should have conceived a burning desire to follow in such steps, and carry the art of healing the body as well as the soul into those distant lands and among those ignorant suffering races, in the direction of which his studies and his natural sympathies had gradually tended.

Livingstone was about nineteen years of age when he determined to prepare for the life of a medical missionary, and it is again characteristic of his nationality that he should have set about this task, infinitely more difficult then than now, without seeking aid or influence from any person or society. He was by this time a "spinner," and the wages he earned in summer sufficed to support him in winter at the neighbouring city of Glasgow, whither he went to get the benefit of the Greek, divinity, and medical lectures of its university. His first session was in the winter of 1836-37, and on its conclusion he returned to his labour at the Blantyre mill.

It was not without the strictest economy that David was enabled to go through even the economical course of a Scotch university. We can gather some idea of his style of housekeeping in the University City, when we remember that his lodgings cost him no more than half-a-crown a week, and that, in common with other Scotch students, he lived largely on oatmeal. Yet, even with this sparing diet and modest establishment, it is on record that he was unable to enter on the second session without pecuniary help from his elder brother—help, be it noted, which was scrupulously repaid. Such help would have been unneeded had Livingstone been only studying theology, for the expenses of training as a missionary pure and simple were comparatively light; but he had the twofold object in view of tending both body and soul, and the medical fees were a heavy drain upon his slender purse.

It is evident that during the two years at Glasgow, Livingstone largely developed the scientific side of his nature. His very liberality in theology was owing to his perfectly impartial method of testing every question. Had he been more of a theologian, it is quite conceivable he might have lost much of that primitive Christian spirit which marked his whole life, and without doubt contributed largely to his success in dealing with the raw African. He has told us himself that, when he was advised to join the London Missionary Society, he was attracted by its "perfectly unsectarian character." "It sends," he wrote, "neither episcopacy, nor presbyterianism, nor independency, but the Gospel of Christ, to the heathen. This," he adds, "exactly agreed with my ideas of what a missionary society ought to do." And in the course of this book it will be shown how exactly such ideas were clothed in his own missionary life, for to the very end he never ceased to claim forbearance toward the ignorant or the hostile, and tolerance toward all.

The friends of his university years will be found, then, not among the classmates of the theological school, but among those of the medical and scientific. Perhaps his greatest friend, certainly the most constant, was James Young, who afterwards devoted his attainments in chemistry to the purification of petroleum, and won for his name the familiarity of a household word, as well as from Livingstone the jocular title of "Sir Paraffin." Dr. Graham, the Professor of Chemistry, and Dr. Andrew Buchanan, of the Medical Faculty, were also great and kind friends. Sir Lyon Playfair was another classmate and friend; and those two great scientists, Professors James Thomson and Sir William Thomson, were others.

During his second session at Glasgow (1837-38), Livingstone forwarded his application to the London Missionary Society, and, as it contains a clear definition of his views of a missionary's duty, it will be well to quote a portion of it here. "The missionary's object," he wrote, "is to endeavour, by every means in his power, to make known the Gospel by preaching, exhortation, conversation, instruction of the young; improving, so far as in his power, the temporal condition of those among whom he labours, by introducing the arts and sciences of civilization, and doing everything to commend Christianity to their hearts and consciences." For the first part of this definition he was preparing by study and practical piety—by " plain living and high thinking;" and for the second by picking up as much of carpentry and other useful trades as possible. Without some such wise anticipation as this, he would have been sadly puzzled when a few years afterwards he was confronted with the task of building both dwelling-house and school-house and cultivating grain and roots for his own sustenance on his mission-station.

A great clue to all Livingstone's actions, both at this time and throughout the whole of his after-life—especially when his geographical labours in Africa were regarded with disapprobation by many men of pious life but narrow views—is to be found in the independence of his character. It came out forcibly at his final examination for the Diploma of Licentiate of Faculty of Physicians and Surgeons. He says: "Between me and the examiners a slight difference of opinion existed as to whether this instrument (the stethoscope) could do what was asserted. . . . I unwittingly procured for myself an examination rather more severe and prolonged than usual among examining bodies. . . . However, I was admitted. . . . It was with unfeigned delight I became a member of a profession which is pre-eminently devoted to practical benevolence, and which with unwearied energy pursues from age to age its endeavours to lessen human woe."

The London Missionary Society had accepted his offer provisionally, and in September 1838 Livingstone went to London in order to interview the heads of that Society. He was then sent to the Rev. Richard Cecil, of Chipping Ongar, Essex, and with several other candidates received theological and pastoral instruction from that gentleman. His preaching capacity appeared to be slight, and, as an unfavourable report was sent in to the society, it was by the merest chance that he was accepted. Some one pleaded in his favour; he was given another opportunity, and finally his services were engaged. There can be no doubt, however, that an adverse decision would have had no effect upon Livingstone's plans. Indeed, such was his independence, he would probably have relished going out to preach and civilize the heathen under the ægis of no authorized body far more than as the accredited agent of one. And, as a matter of fact, it will be seen later that, when a difficulty arose, Livingstone severed his connection with the Society rather than embarrass its position or his own.

The years of preparation were now drawing to a close, and the question of "Whither?" faced the young missionary. In his own mind it had been settled for some time; his eyes had been fixed on China and its enormous and untilled harvest field for several years. It was with the special intention of dealing with the exclusive people of that country that he had determined on becoming a doctor, and it was therefore a great blow to his hopes when the opium war broke out between that country and Great Britain, and effectually closed China to the European. For a while his destination was uncertain; but a meeting with Robert Moffat, who had lately returned to England from his mission in South Africa, led Livingstone to determine on that almost unknown region as the scene of his future labours. Dr. Moffat has left an account of this meeting, which has a special interest in the light of the lifelong connection which was to unite the two men, and a portion of it may be quoted here.

"He asked me whether I thought he would do for Africa. I said I believed he would, if he would not go to an old station, but would advance to unoccupied ground, specifying the vast plain to the north, where I had sometimes seen, in the morning sun, the smoke of a thousand villages, where no missionary had ever been. At last Livingstone said: 'What is the use of my waiting for the end of this abominable opium war? I will go at once to Africa!' The Directors concurred, and Africa became his sphere."

Livingstone had been studying both theology and medicine in London for some time, and toward the end of 1840 he returned to Glasgow, and obtained that medical diploma to which reference has already been made. He was now therefore equipped for the fight, and with the ardour of his nature was willing and anxious for service. He had not long to wait. Within a few days he received the summons, and on the 17th of November bade farewell to his relatives and friends, and returned to London. His father, for whom he had both affection and respect, he was never to see again. Sixteen years later, when Livingstone was winning glory in the heart of Africa, the old man died, but not before he had heard with pride and thankfulness of his son's achievements. In simple language that son has written a beautiful elegy upon him, closing with these pregnant words: "I revere his memory."

On the 20th of November, in Albion Street Chapel, Livingstone received his formal commission to preach the Word. Less than a month afterwards, he was sailing southward on the Atlantic, bound for the Cape of Good Hope.

MISSIONARY STATION, KURUMAN.

CHAPTER II.

EARLY YEARS IN AFRICA.

DAVID LIVINGSTONE had received general orders from the Society to proceed first to Kuruman, the headquarters of the Moffats, and then to advance northward into the interior. He was bearing with him five hundred copies of Moffat's Sechwana New Testament, just printed under the veteran missionary's personal supervision in England, and was looking forward with eagerness to the day when he could strike out into the new region set apart for his labours.

At this time Kuruman was the most northerly missionary station in South Africa, or, as Livingstone chose to put it, "the most southern point of the real missionary field." About seven hundred miles northeast of Capetown, and at that time more usually reached from Port Elizabeth, Kuruman was situated close to the source of the Kuruman River, which, flowing in a north-westerly direction for about two hundred miles, and then almost due south for the same distance, ultimately entered the Orange River, the most important of South African rivers. To the south-west of Kuruman lay Griqualand and its Boer population; to the south-east, across the Vaal, the Orange River Free State, with a similar population. From the station northward stretched tribe after tribe of Bechwanas, who passed by many different names. At Kuruman itself they were Batlapis; a little farther to the north and north-west, Bangwaketse; some two hundred miles to the north, Bakwains; and beyond these again, the Bakaa. Northward of the Bechwanas was Matabeleland, and beyond that the Zambesi. The route into the interior lay through these tribes; for on the west the missionary was hemmed in by the waterless Kalahari desert, and on the east by the unfriendly Boers.

Little had as yet been achieved among the native tribes lying along this route; for, although Robert Moffat had made many journeys and had lived for months at a time among various tribes of the Bechwanas, and had even penetrated to Matabeleland and made its great chief, Moselekatse, who lived on the western slopes of the mountain ridge which formed the eastern boundary of his country, a staunch personal friend, his life's work had centred in Kuruman and the straggling population around.

Kuruman, in fact, was the only place for a hundred miles round where Europeans could settle and exist. And even at Kuruman the excessive droughts which are the curse of the greater part of South Africa were not unknown. Bechwanaland was essentially a dry country—so dry, indeed, that Livingstone has told us that needles could be left for months exposed to the outer air without rusting. To grow crops with success irrigation was necessary, and Moffatt had won the confidence of the natives by his active exertions to procure by this means security for the harvest. He had thus taken the professional "rain-makers"—his most active opponents—in the rear, and enabled the wretched natives to dispense with the services of these soothsayers. By striking this blow at the most influential interpreters of the old superstitions, he had paved the way to a reception of the tidings it was his mission to bring.

When Livingstone arrived at Kuruman, he found affairs in a prospering condition. From a few Hottentot servants the Christian congregation had increased to about a thousand, the mission-house and church had been rebuilt on a larger scale and of stone, the schools had become flourishing institutions, and the advance of civilization was marked by those of the natives who could afford it purchasing waggons and using oxen for labour in the place of women. "The gardens," wrote Livingstone, "irrigated by the Kuruman rivulet, are well stocked with fruit trees and vines, and yield European vegetables and grain readily. The pleasantness of the place is enhanced by the contrast it presents to the surrounding scenery, and the fact that it owes all its beauty to the manual labour of the missionaries. Externally it presents a picture of civilized comfort to the adjacent tribes; and by its printing-press . . . the light of Christianity is gradually diffused in the surrounding region."

It must be remembered that all this was not attained without much labour and hardship. For twenty years the Moffats had laboured on the banks of the Kuruman before they began to gather in the harvest or entered into the reward of their labours. As Livingstone stood in this oasis, he saw the desert widening and lengthening before him; his years of toil and anxiety were all to come. Would they, too, bring a like accomplishment? We shall see.

While awaiting the permission of the Society to erect a mission-station north of Kuruman, Livingstone was journeying up and down the whole Bechwana country. He visited the Bakwains—whose chief, Sechéle, became a great friend—the Bamangwato, the Bakaa, and the Bakhatla in succession, studying their language and customs, and in every way equipping himself for useful effort amongst them. In the meanwhile he was taking careful notes of the adaptability of the country to agriculture, inquiring into the causes of its intense dryness, and making up his mind even at this early date as to the right method of evangelizing Africa. It speaks much for his perspicacity that the opinions he then formed he never saw cause to surrender. He wrote home to the Directors of the Society with his usual emphatic independence, pointing out how necessary it was to draw men away from the straggling population between Capetown and Kuruman, and scatter them throughout the more densely-peopled country to the north of that outpost; in fact, how necessary it was for the Society to reverse its policy. Undervaluing their young representative, and rejecting, for a time at least, what would naturally seem the over-sanguine views of an inexperienced missionary, the Society made no further move than to send their permission for the founding of a new station.

It was not until late in the year 1843 that Livingstone was able to move northward, and establish his first station in Africa in a pleasant valley leading from a mountain range, which the Bakhatla called Mabotsa. By this name also the station came to be known.

Shortly after his arrival, he met with that encounter with a lion which is perhaps one of the most familiar events of his life. Struck to the ground by the beast in his spring, his flesh torn and the upper bone of his arm crunched in the lion's mouth, Livingstone was only saved from death by the courageous conduct of a faithful servant, who was also a native deacon. In his attempt to rescue his master, Mebalwe nearly lost his own life; for the lion quitted his hold of Livingstone's arm, dashed blindly at Mebalwe, biting him on the thigh, and then, while in the act of attacking another native, fell dead from the bullets he had received. Livingstone's comment on this is characteristic: "But for the importunities of friends, I meant to have kept (this story) in store to tell my children when in my dotage."

As soon as his arm was healed, he set about building the mission-house and school-house, and in converting the ground adjacent into a garden. Before long he found cause for enlarging his house, for in one of his visits to Kuruman he capped a fond attachment to Mary, the eldest child of the Moffats, by proposing marriage and being accepted. Mary Moffat soon afterwards became Mary Livingstone, and the two settled down to a busy life among the Bakhatla.

The life before the Doctor appeared to him to be projected on similar lines to that which the veteran Moffat had been leading for so many years, though somewhat extended in usefulness and influence, perhaps, by his greater medical skill. He was, moreover, determined to put into practice his cherished theory of training natives for the ministry, for on this point he was always very decided; and it is not surprising, considering the havoc fever had played with the Europeans, and the difficulty, the impossibility, of procuring them in sufficient numbers to grapple with the vast population of the interior. But neither this nor the settled life of Moffat was to fall to his lot. He was reserved for a greater and more difficult work.

He had not been long at Mabotsa when, through some absurd jealously, his fellow missionary accused him of overstepping his rights and claiming to act with greater freedom and irresponsibility than his position as a brother missionary entitled him to. This weak brother circulated his fancied wrongs and suppression among the missionaries at the Cape, and even wrote

"STRUCK TO THE GROUND BY THE BEAST IN HIS SPRING."

home to the Society. Livingstone was naturally indignant, but said little. He gave up the house he had built with his own hands and the garden he had created by his own toil, and left them generously in the possession of his enemy. Turning his back upon Mabotsa, he marched some forty miles northward to Chonuane, the capital of the Bakwains, and the residence of their chief, Sechéle. Here he founded his second station.

The task of building and cultivating began again, but he was cheered in his labour by the firm friendship of Sechéle. After three years of instruction and probation the chief received baptism. But the people still hung back. The country was suffering from one of those fearful South African droughts of which the European can have no conception, and the people were told by the baffled "rain-makers" that Livingstone had bewitched the rain, and none would come to rescue their crops from failure or themselves from ruin unless the missionary was sent away. Even Sechéle complained, in characteristic language, of the backwardness of his people in following his example. "In former times," said he, "when a chief was fond of hunting, all his people got dogs and became fond of hunting too. If he was fond of dancing or music, all showed a liking in these amusements too. If the chief loved beer, they all rejoiced in strong drink. But in this case it is different. I love the Word of God, and not one of my brethren will join me."

Some progress, however, had been made, for the Day of Rest was generally observed, and in secular matters the people recognised in the missionary a friend. The drought and the hunger it entailed were prime factors in their reluctance to embrace the new religion. They still hoped success would attend the incantations of the rain-makers. They hoped in vain.

Livingstone soon came to the conclusion that the only chance of missionary success and prosperity for the tribe amongst whom he had cast his lot was to move to a more favoured region; and Sechéle and his people being nothing loth, the whole community moved westward to the river Kolobeng, about forty miles distant. Under Livingstone's direction canals and trenches were cut in connection with the river, and a complete system of irrigation introduced. Sechéle built the school-house at his own expense, and Livingstone once more had to make a home. "Our house," he says, "at the river Kolobeng, which gave a name to the settlement, was the third which I had reared with my own hands. A native smith taught me to weld iron; and, having improved by scraps of information in that line from Mr. Moffat, and also in carpentering and gardening, I was becoming handy at almost any trade, besides doctoring and preaching; and, as my wife could make candles, soap, and clothes, we came nearly up to what may be considered as indispensable in the accomplishments of a missionary family in Central Africa, namely, the husband to be a jack-of-all-trades without doors, and the wife a maid-of-all-work within."

In the midst of his many labours he found time to write home to friends and scientific men. His long letters were marvellous specimens of careful writing and close reasoning, dealing with all the geographical and scientific bearings of the various phenomena he was daily encountering, and ever and again reverting to his views on the missionary subject. He always considered that many of our missionaries who were living fairly comfortable lives in Cape Colony could have been spared for the nobler work among the populous Bechwana and the tribes of the interior. Indeed, his view of the case is very well summed up in a letter to a friend: "If you meet me down in the Colony before eight years are expired, you may shoot me."

At Mabotsa, the Doctor had come in contact with

the Boers, and during his comparatively long residence at Kolobeng he made several journeys eastward into their country. The Boers, who had gradually retreated into the interior as the English extended their sphere of influence, treated the Bechwanas with the same cruelty and contempt they had meted out to the coast Kaffirs. Indeed, their chief grievance against the English was that they had the same law for the black as for the white. The Boers therefore regarded the missionaries with undisguised hatred, and resisted every attempt made to found a mission near their own settlements.

For Livingstone they conceived intense animosity, seeing in him a doughty champion of the ill-used Bechwanas. They accused him of selling guns and gunpowder to the natives; for, although they saw no harm in wantonly massacring whole villages of Bakwains or Bakhatlas, they naturally objected to the possibility of the tables being turned upon themselves. Spies were sent to discover the armed strength of Sechéle's men and the mode of Livingstone's life. They could discover nothing of the atrocities they had imagined, and so they concluded that the missionary had taught the "black property" the arts of deception along with those of civilization. Indeed, the influence of the Boers was such—and for the matter of that the Dutch vote is still an important factor in South African politics—that Livingstone was for a time considered, even at the headquarters of Government at Capetown, to be a highly active and mischievous person!

It is more pleasing to turn from the consideration of these "Africanders" to a look at Livingstone in his daily life and labour. He has left us a vivid picture, too full of detail for insertion here. Everything he required he had to make from the raw material; there were no manufacturers or "middlemen" at Kolobeng. "You want bricks to build a house," he tells us, "and must forthwith proceed to the field, cut down a tree, and saw it into planks to make the brick moulds; the materials for doors and windows, too, are standing in the forest; and, if you want to be respected by the natives, a house of decent dimensions, costing an immense amount of manual labour, must be built." He tells us further on that every brick and stick of the three large houses he had built had to be put square by his own hand.

The bread was almost always baked in an oven which was a hole in the ground; butter was churned in a jar; candles made in wooden moulds; and soap procured from the ashes of a plant. Livingstone does not forget to pay a tribute to his wife—a valuable helpmeet. He wrote in his first published book: " Married life is all the sweeter when so many comforts emanate directly from the thrifty, striving housewife's hands."

After breakfasting early—about six o'clock—Livingstone and his wife taught men, women, and children in school. School over, Mrs. Livingstone attended to domestic duties, while her husband worked as smith, carpenter, or gardener for himself or his people. After dinner, and an hour's *siesta*, his wife taught the infants to sing and the girls to sew. Three nights a week a religious service was held, and on the other evenings Livingstone walked about the settlement, conversing with any and all who might have questions to ask him. Tending the sick and ministering to the diseased, they tried to gain the affections of the natives by supplying the wants of the body. "Show kind attention," says Livingstone, "to the reckless opponents of Christianity on the bed of sickness and pain, and they never can become your personal enemies. Here, if anywhere, love begets love."

The first season had passed away successfully at Kolobeng, owing to the irrigation works, but the drought proved too much for their slender source in the second year, and the river Kolobeng shrank to a mere rivulet. During the whole of the second and third years but ten inches of rain fell, and the fourth year was but little better. The river entirely disappeared, and its bed had to be literally mined in order to procure moisture for the more precious fruit-trees. Pasturage for cattle failed, and the cows gave no milk; the tribe was in a bad way, and became restless again. The restlessness seemed infectious; for Livingstone, whose eyes looked ever northward, and who longed for power to disseminate native deacons and schoolmasters among the people of the interior, made up his mind that Kolobeng, too, must be left behind, and that pastures new and more desirable must be sought. If the natives could not live at Kolobeng, it was very evident that Europeans could not either, and the sooner a new station was selected the better for the tribe among which he was living, and the better also for the prosperity of his Gospel preaching.

In all his plans not one thought occurred of retreating, as he easily might have done, to the Colony, and living in comparative ease and perfect security. No; his eyes were looking fearlessly northward, and his whole soul breathed the one word "Onward!"

AN AFRICAN VILLAGE.

CHAPTER III.

MISSIONARY TRAVELS.

LITTLE did Livingstone think that when he left Kolobeng to seek a more suitable settlement for himself and his friends the Bakwains, he was really entering on a career of travel and exploration which was to place his name on the highest pinnacle of fame and only end with his death.

Yet such was the case, and therefore it cannot but be appropriate to consider here, as briefly as possible, the twofold position of Livingstone as a missionary and an explorer.

It is evident enough that, when he left his wife and three children at Kolobeng, his sole purpose was to seek the country of Sebituane, and ascertain if the regions of the " great lake " of which he had so often heard were healthful and suitable to missionary enterprise. In his efforts to preach the Gospel to the various tribes he encountered, he found it after a while impossible to take his family with him, and reluctantly he consented to their departure to England. At once set free from all family responsibility, he entered into those wider labours which ultimately led him across the continent of Africa. This was no mere effort of geographical enterprise, but undertaken in a purely humanitarian spirit. He had by that time discovered the growing enormity of the slave trade, which prospered wherever the Arabs, coast tribes, and Portuguese had access; and to stamp this out became one of the ruling passions of his life. With a statesmanlike appreciation of the case, he saw that if he could foster legitimate trade that in human flesh would probably subside. If the tribes of the interior had nothing to exchange for those cottons and guns, bright tinsel ornaments, beads and wire, which were displayed so temptingly before their eyes, and which they naturally coveted, but the men, women, and children they had captured in their tribal wars, or, failing these, even their own kith and kin, then, as Livingstone saw plainly, their uncontrolled greed would lead them to trade in slaves. In his anxiety to suppress this growing traffic, he sought an outlet for such raw material as the natives could be induced to gather. His search for some great natural highway to the ocean led him first to Loanda on the west coast, and then from there to Quilimane on the shores of the Indian Ocean.

Yet all the while he hungered for the soul of the African. It has already been mentioned that he believed far more could be effected by native agencies than by European; that the vast needs of Africa could only be met by raising up a suitable supply from the practically inexhaustible material at hand. His views, however, differed from the accepted ideas of missionary labour. Projected over a series of years and much toil, they revealed the true proportion and perspective of events and efforts. He became convinced—and to be convinced with Livingstone was to be enthusiastic as well—that the evangelizing of Africa was not to be achieved in its earliest stage by building stations and settling permanently among one people; but rather by staying a few years with each tribe, preaching the Gospel, specially instructing such as would receive it, and then moving on to new tribes. " Our own elevation," he said, " has been the work of centuries; and, remembering this, we should not indulge in overwrought expectations as to the elevation which those who have inherited the degradation of ages may attain in our day."

And so it happened that, whenever and wherever he travelled in the years to come, he sowed the seed as he went. Far and wide he flung it; and far and wide, even to this day, his name is remembered with respect. The principle which actuated him through it all is contained in those well-known words of his: " The end of the geographical feat is only the beginning of the missionary enterprise."

On the 1st of June, 1849, and in company with two Englishmen bent on sporting adventure—Mr. Oswell and Mr. Murray—Livingstone set out on his northward march. Right in his track lay the great Kalahari Desert. From the Orange River in the south to Lake Ngami in the north, from the Transvaal on the east to Great Namaqualand on the west, this vast tract of country extends—in its southern portions open and grassy, and in its northern wooded as well. It is flat and sandy, and in many parts grass grows luxuriantly, and bushes and trees are not uncommon. Here and there are distinctly traceable the beds of ancient rivers, but no water ever flows along them now. It is a region of few wells and no streams, a country of complete drought; and to the natives and Boers who dwelt east of it, the Kalahari Desert conveyed the idea of utter desolation.

And yet this idea was in many respects erroneous. Large numbers of Bushmen lead a nomadic life upon this sandy plain. From place to place they follow the antelope—a beast which resembles the camel in his ability to dispense with water—as he roams, one of enormous herds, across the "desert." The natives eat of the scarlet cucumbers and the succulent water-melons which in many districts carpet the ground; and they drink of the water-bearing tubers which, found a foot or so below the surface of the soil, produce a liquor of surprising coolness. And just as the slight and wiry physique of the Bushman is adapted in no common measure to his local environment, so are many plants found which are here, and nowhere else, provided with tuber-reservoirs at a depth below the ground sufficient to preserve life and ensure growth. Animals which are usually regarded as carnivorous become herbivorous in the presence of that "date-palm" of the Kalahari, the water-melon. For not only do the elephant and rhinoceros delight in it, but the jackal, the hyæna, and even the lion himself, eat of it readily. In short, despite the monotony of the vegetation and the absolute want of surface water, the Kalahari Desert supports a large population, numerous animals, fruits of several kinds in great quantity, and in many parts an abundance of grass. Hostile in aspect, it has a not unkindly heart: yet its character is such that the stranger may die where the native would find enough and to spare.

After travelling for about a month, suffering at times a good deal from thirst, and being deceived at others by the glittering salt-pans which appeared through mirage to be lakes or rivers, Livingstone and his party reached the Zouga River. From this point to the Ngami Lake the route was comparatively easy; the river ran a south-easterly course from the lake, and they had but to follow the river.

It was while ascending the Zouga that Livingstone first discovered the nature of the region which is generally called South Central Africa. That vast plateau of sand, which "arm-chair geographers" had decided was the true character of this region, disappeared for ever when Livingstone inquired into the source of the Tamanakle, an affluent of the Zouga, and asked from what sort of land it came. The answer that was given him was this: "From a country full of rivers—so many no one can tell their number—and full of large trees!" That answer opened up such a vista before him that Livingstone declared, on at last sighting the much-talked-of lake, that its discovery seemed of little importance! He was already, in spirit, travelling upon the waterways, and reposing under the umbrageous forest trees of the Zambesi basin.

On the 1st of August the lake was sighted at its north-east end. It has proved to have, usually, an area of three hundred square miles; but, like some other African lakes, it largely expands and contracts in accordance with the wet or the dry season. When the lake is full, the water is fresh; when low, it is brackish. To-day it may be deep in almost every part; three months hence a canoe might be punted over its bosom for miles at a time.

Livingstone's chief object in coming north was to visit Sebituane, the powerful chief of a great people—the Makololo. This individual had been very kind in former years to Sechéle, Livingstone's old ally, and it was with the idea of migrating to the country of the Makololo that the missionary had left Kolobeng for the court of Sebituane. He was, however, prevented from advancing beyond Ngami by the jealousy of Lechulatebe, the most important chief on the shores of the lake. He refused to transport the party across the Zouga, and the determination of Livingstone nearly cost him his life. "Trying hard," he wrote in his journal, "to form a raft at a narrow part, I worked many hours in the water; but the dry wood was so worm-eaten it would not bear the weight of a single person. I was not then aware of the number of alligators which exist in the Zouga, and never think of my labour in the water without feeling thankful that I escaped their jaws."

Descending the Zouga slowly, and taking most careful notes of all animal and vegetable life that met his eyes, Livingstone returned to Kolobeng. In April of the following year, however, he once more started for the lake and Sebituane's. This time he was accompanied by his wife and three children, as well as by Sechéle. On arriving at Lechulatebe's he lost no time in again pressing his wish to be allowed to proceed to Sebituane's, and had just gained his point and obtained the promise of substantial help when an unforeseen occurrence upset all his plans. Two of his children and most of his servants were prostrated with fever, and an immediate departure became necessary. But it was to the comparatively pure air of the more elevated Kalahari that Livingstone took his party: his departure, in fact, was a retreat. The low-lying country round the lake was eminently unhealthy, and with slow steps and a sad heart Livingstone returned once more to Kolobeng.

Here a fourth child was born—only to be swept away by an epidemic prevalent at the time. Livingstone wrote: "It was the first death in our family. . . . We felt her loss keenly. . . . It is wonderful how soon the affections twine round a little stranger." Soon afterwards Mrs. Livingstone had a severe illness; and, her husband being also in poor health, for the sake of change the whole party journeyed to Kuruman, where in the delightful home which the efforts of Robert Moffat had created they gathered strength for future effort.

In April 1851 a third, and this time a successful, attempt was made to gain the country of the Makololo. The route lay across the worst part of the Kalahari Desert, and more than once death from thirst appeared imminent. When water became more frequent, another danger appeared. The children were so savagely attacked by mosquitoes, that for a long time they were in a highly feverish state. When the children seemed improving, a new cause for alarm arose in the appearance of the tse-tse fly, which threatened to destroy the cattle, their sole means of transport. So great a part has this fly played in African exploration, that a brief description of it may well be given here.

In size about that of the common house fly, and in colour that of the honey-bee, this small and insignificant-looking insect is nevertheless terribly powerful. On this journey alone Livingstone lost forty-three oxen from its bite, and they were watched so carefully that he believed hardly a score of flies had ever settled on them. Fatal as is its bite on the horse, ox, or dog, it has no effect upon man, the mule, or goat, or upon wild animals. In the act of biting, the middle prong of the triple proboscis first pierces the skin, and then is partly withdrawn while the mandibles set to work. When the fly has had its fill, it brings its large wings into action and goes away. An irritation supervenes, and in the case of man shortly subsides. In the ox, however, after a few days the poison has reached a high state of activity. Catarrh occurs at the eyes and nose, and in some parts a slight swelling arises. After this the muscles become flaccid, the animal rapidly emaciated, and it ultimately dies of exhaustion. Sometimes, if the bitten ox be in superior condition, the poison goes to the brain, producing blindness and "staggers," and comparatively sudden death.

The symptoms which the organs of animals so destroyed present are those of blood-poisoning, and the poison of the tse-tse is contained in a bulb at the root of the proboscis. The quantity, however, is so minute that it has been supposed that it has the property of reproduction in the animal. At any rate the influence of the tse-tse on horses and oxen is such that any one who trusts to them for the transport of himself through a difficult country will do his very utmost to avoid the well-defined localities which the fly affects.

At last Livingstone reached the court of Sebituane, and looked on the face of the man whose name was the most widely known and feared throughout the region between the Cape Colony and the Zambesi. He was a man in the prime of life, tall and strong, of an olive colour, and "more frank in his answers than any other chief I ever met." His career had been a chequered one, and it was due to his great courage and ability that he had won for himself the position he held as chief of the warlike Makololo. He received Livingstone most warmly, and it was a keen sorrow to the latter and a great blow to his hopes when Sebituane died within a month of his arrival.

Sebituane was succeeded by Mamochisane, his daughter, and she gave Livingstone and Oswell permission to go anywhere they pleased throughout her country. They at once marched northward to find the great river of which the natives had spoken, and at the end of June 1851 their search was rewarded at Sesheke by the discovery of the Zambesi in the heart of Africa.

This was a discovery of great geographical importance, besides bearing directly on Livingstone's cherished scheme of finding and opening routes to the oceans on either hand. Up to this time the very existence of the river in the longitude of Sesheke was unknown. The Portuguese, who held the coast on the east and the west, were the people most likely to know the extent of the Zambesi; but with few exceptions the Portuguese have been, during the last century or so, only less disinclined to exploration than to missionary enterprise. Their maps, consequently, placed the sources of the Zambesi far to the east of even Sesheke! And yet this is what Livingstone says of the river at that point, and in the dry season:—

"The river was at its lowest, and yet there was a breadth of from three hundred to six hundred yards of deep flowing water. At the period of its annual inundation it rises fully twenty feet in perpendicular height, and floods fifteen or twenty miles of lands adjacent to its banks."

The one idea which possessed Livingstone now was to gauge the extent of this vast highway for commerce and civilization; to trace it to its sources, to follow it to the coast. He could not, however, do this with his family; neither could he leave them in the swampy region between the Chobe and the Zambesi, where the Makololo were then living; neither could he send them back to Kolobeng, as the Boers were not likely to leave them in peace there. So he determined, as he has told us, to part from them for a time. "I at once resolved to save my family from exposure to this unhealthy region by sending them to England, and to return alone, with a view to exploring the country in search of a healthy district that might prove a centre of civilization and open up the interior by a path to the east or west coast."

He accordingly took his family to the Cape, and for the first time after a lapse of eleven years came in contact with civilized life. The absence was to be for two years; before they met again five years had passed, and Livingstone, from being an unknown missionary in Bechwanaland, had leaped into world-wide fame by his famous journey to Loanda, and thence across Africa.

While Livingstone was slowly returning to Kolobeng, the Boers attacked the Bakwains, slew many, and took more away into captivity. His own house was sacked, the furniture carried away, and all the books of his valued library torn to pieces, and the leaves scattered on the ground outside his house. Enormous numbers of cattle were raided, and the children of Sechéle, the chief, stolen. It was fortunate for Livingstone that he

was not at Kolobeng, for Pretorius had threatened to kill him, and there can be little doubt that that threat would have been carried out. There was not the shadow of justification for this and other murderous incursions of the Boers; and as Livingstone subsequently and shrewdly pointed out, if the Bakwains had been producers of raw material for English commerce, the outrageous conduct of the Boers would not have gone unpunished, not to mention unheeded, by the English nation. And he adds: "We ought to encourage the Africans to cultivate for our markets, as the most effectual means, next to the Gospel, of their elevation."

As directly assisting to this end, he became more than ever determined to open up the interior—the Boer policy being one of exclusiveness. So after some delay, owing to the unsettled state of the country, he procured guides, and arrived safely at Linyanti, the chief town of the Makololo people, in the month of June, 1853. It will be remembered that during his last visit he had found the country swampy and unhealthy. This second visit not only confirmed his opinion that the climate was most hurtful to Europeans, but he also discovered that many parts of the country were almost impassable. Livingstone speaks of lofty grass "which at certain angles cut the hands like a razor," and which was so welded into mass by climbing convolvuli, that often the only way progress could be made was by two or three men leaning against a part and bending it down till they could stand on and walk over it! When to this sort of vegetation is added the fact that for miles and miles the country was in flood—stagnant rather than current—the difficulties of travel and the obstacles to the active work of civilization become more obvious.

Mamochisane, the daughter of the old chief Sebituane, appeared to have found the cares of government too much for her, for she had handed them over to her brother, Sekeletu. By this young man Livingstone was cordially received and assisted in his various plans. He remained for some months with the Makololo, preaching the Gospel continually, and treating with medical skill those cases which the native doctors had given up in despair. He was so attracted by the manly spirit and hospitable ways exhibited by this race, that one time he had almost made up his mind to settle amongst them. But the extreme unhealthiness of the climate, from which he was suffering much, deterred him from this step, and led him on in his search after a healthful district where Europeans could settle permanently, and from which trained native teachers might be sent out in all directions—rays of light to illumine this desperately dark region.

On the 11th of November, 1853, Livingstone set out on the journey which was to end at Loanda. He had sent his companions back to Kuruman and the Cape, and took with him instead twenty-seven men whom Sekeletu provided. These men, Livingstone said, might have been called Zambesians, for there were only two true Makololo among them.

In these latter days of exploring Africa with elaborate equipments and large armed forces, Livingstone's outfit is worth noting. For food he took "only a few biscuits, a few pounds of tea and sugar, and about twenty of coffee." Of clothing he had some in a small tin box for use on reaching the civilized towns on the coast; of books he had three—a Bible, a Nautical Almanac, and Thomson's Logarithm Tables. Of course he had his journal with him—a toughly bound book of more than eight hundred pages. His stock of medicines was enclosed in a tin box, and the precious sextant, thermometer, and compasses were carried separately. For his followers he had three muskets, for himself a rifle and double-barrelled gun. The only use the ammunition was to be put to was the provision of food; and, failing the presence of game, about twenty pounds of beads were taken to purchase food from the natives. Livingstone's bed was a horse-rug, his blanket a sheep-skin. The sole protection he afforded himself from tempestuous weather was represented by a small gipsy tent. One more item remains to be noticed. He had been given by Mr. Murray a magic-lantern with slides of Scripture scenes, and this always afforded entertainment to the various audiences he met in his journey. "It was," he wrote, "the only mode of instruction I was ever pressed to repeat."

After crossing the river Chobe, and following its left bank for some distance, Livingstone arrived at Sesheke, where for the second time he beheld the "great river"—the Zambesi, or Leeambye, as it was called by the natives. He proceeded in a north-westerly direction along the bank of this river, until he reached its confluence with the Leeba. Here the Leeambye, or Zambesi, branched off in a north-easterly direction, away from the course he had determined to follow. The bank of the Leeba, which issued from Lake Dilolo, in the country of Lunda, in the north-west, consequently became his route. On arriving at the lake, he travelled across the country of the Basonge, over the elevated ridges, which increased in height and grandeur as he pressed forward; and ultimately, on the 31st of May, 1854, he arrived at Loanda, the chief town of the Portuguese settlements on the west coast.

A few extracts from the Doctor's journal will give a glimpse of the various scenes he encountered in this march from Linyanti to Loanda, and enable the reader to realise to a slight extent some of the many difficulties and novelties which lay in his path:

"The forests became more dense as we went north. We travelled much more in the deep gloom of the forest than in open sunlight. Large climbing plants entwined themselves around the trunks and branches of gigantic trees like boa-constrictors; and they often do constrict the trees by which they rise, and, killing them, stand erect themselves. There were other trees quite new to my companions; many of them ran up to a height of fifty feet of one thickness and without branches.

"There was considerable pleasure, in spite of rain and fever, in this new scenery. The deep gloom contrasted strongly with the shadeless glare of the Kalahari, which has left an indelible impression on my memory. Though drenched day by day at this time and for months afterwards, it was long before I could believe that we were getting too much of a good thing. Nor could I look at water being thrown away without a slight, quick impression flitting across the mind that we were guilty of wasting it.

"The number of little villages seemed about equal to the number of valleys. . . . Every village had its idols near it. This is the case all through the country of the Balonda; so that, when we came to an idol in the woods, we always knew that we were within a quarter of an hour of human habitations.

"We came to a most lovely valley about a mile and a half wide. A small stream meanders down the centre of this pleasant green glen; and on a little rill which flows into it from the western side stands the town of Kabompo—or, as he likes best to be called, Shinte. We found the town embowered in banana and other tropical trees having great expansion of leaf. . . . Here we first saw native huts with square walls and round roofs. The fences or walls of the courts which surround the huts are wonderfully straight, and made of upright poles a few inches apart, with strong grass or leafy bushes neatly woven between. In the courts were small plantations of tobacco and a little solanaceous plant which these Balonda use as a relish; also sugar and bananas."

When interviewing one of the chiefs, "I introduced the subject of the Bible; but one of the old councillors broke in, told all he had picked up from the Mambari, and glided off into several other subjects. It is a misery to speak through an interpreter, as I was now forced to do. With a body of men like mine, composed as they were of six different tribes, and all speaking the language of the Bechwanas, there was no difficulty in communicating on common subjects with any tribe we came to; but doling out a story in which they felt no interest, and which I understood only sufficiently well to perceive that a mere abridgment was given, was uncommonly slow work."

Throughout this journey Livingstone suffered greatly from fever, and he arrived at Loanda a mere "bag of bones," so reduced was his frame by the constant recurrence of the malaria. Here is a remark which shows that he suffered from more than the actual disease: "On Sunday, the 19th, both I and several of our party were seized with fever, and I could do nothing but toss about in my little tent, with the thermometer above 90°, though this was the beginning of winter, and my men made as much shade as possible by planting branches of trees all round and over it. We have, for the first time in my experience in Africa, had a cold wind from the north. All the winds from that quarter are hot, and those from the south are cold; but they seldom blow from either direction."

No wonder was it that Livingstone rejoiced at reaching Loanda at last! His mind worn and depressed by disease and care, his body wasted with fever and chronic dysentery, he was in a position to receive with all the gratitude of a grateful nature the kindness of the one Englishman living in Loanda at that time. This was Mr. Gabriel, the British commissioner for the suppression of the slave trade. "Seeing me ill," wrote Livingstone, "he benevolently offered me his bed. Never shall I forget the luxuriant pleasure I enjoyed in feeling myself again on a good English couch, after six months sleeping on the ground. I was soon asleep!"

AFRICAN BUFFALOES.

CHAPTER IV.

ACROSS AFRICA.

THE journey which had ended successfully at Loanda, in spite of numerous physical difficulties and the extortion and hostility of certain chiefs, had not fulfilled all Livingstone had hoped. The country he had discovered was highly injurious to the health of Europeans, and could not therefore be regarded as suitable for the great mission centre ever before his eyes; and the difficulties of the route precluded its proving an easy and safe high-road from the interior of the continent to the sea. He had still before him the discovery of these two necessities for the development and evangelization of the natives, and to a man of Livingstone's intense conscientiousness this discovery appeared in the light of an immediate duty. Moreover, his faithful Makololo, who had accompanied him for so many hundreds of miles to the shores of the great sea, and who had looked upon the white man's "canoe" in the shape of a British war-vessel, and had declared it to be "no canoe, but a town"—these men could not be allowed to find their way back to Linyanti. Their leader must take them himself.

In the meanwhile, however, that leader was prostrated by a severe attack of fever, lying for long weeks on a bed of sickness, though carefully tended by his fellow-countryman, Mr. Gabriel. On his recovery, Livingstone set about acknowledging the many kindnesses that had been shown him by the Portuguese authorities, and investigating the state of affairs in Loanda and Angola, and the real policy of the government.

The trade in slaves, of which as he had drawn nearer and nearer to the coast he had met increasing traces as well as proofs, was the uppermost idea in his mind. Despite the hospitality and personal courtesy of the Portuguese he encountered at Loanda, he could not but see that the attitude of hostility to the slave trade which they had recently announced was a mere political form, and that the material as well as the personal interests of the officials led them to foster secretly, if not openly, traffic in flesh and blood. Nothing could exceed his gratitude for their kindness to him, but nothing could weaken his firm conviction that many of them had at heart the prosperity of the slave trade.

Although Livingstone was not content with the discoveries he had made on his way from Linyanti, there were not wanting others who viewed his work with the very highest appreciation. The Royal Geographical Society regarded it so favourably, that it awarded him the Patron's Gold Medal. Livingstone, indeed, was not unknown to the society, for it had already made him a grant on his discovery of Lake Ngami.

This last achievement was of great importance; for he had not only passed through entirely new country, taking most elaborate and careful notes of the geographical facts which everywhere presented themselves to him, and entering most fully into considerations on the social fabric of the inhabitants and the capabilities of their environment, but he had also made an enormous number of astronomical calculations, determining his exact route, and vastly enhancing the value of his maps. It was afterwards said in public by his friend Sir Thomas Maclear, the Astronomer-Royal at the Cape, who helped largely by hints and subsequent corrections to make those calculations complete, that he never knew a man who, "knowing scarcely anything of the method of making geographical observations or laying down positions, become so soon an adept. . . . I say, what that man has done is unprecedented. . . . You could go to any point across the entire continent, along Livingstone's track, and feel certain of your position."

These remarks, though partly referring to the work Livingstone had just performed, were made after his journey across the whole width of Africa—a journey he was now to commence. He had taken six months to reach Loanda from Linyanti; the return journey was to occupy just double that time, and six months more were to be spent in actual travelling before he reached Quilimane.

In addition to a new equipment for the arduous work before him, Livingstone took away from Loanda various presents which the officials and merchants sent to Sekeletu.

The Makololo quite realised the benefit that direct trade with the Portuguese on the coast would be to them, and their appreciation of all that they had seen was enhanced by gifts to themselves. On leaving Loanda, Livingstone gave them each a musket, besides taking with him a quantity of cotton cloth and beads, with which to "pay his way." The party was enlarged by several carriers, who were required to convey the increased baggage; and finally, on the 20th of September, 1854, they set out from Loanda, and turned their backs upon "the white man's sea."

The route was almost identical with that which they

had previously followed. Fine ranges of hills flanked the path both northward and southward, and while they were in Angola coffee and cotton plantations were met with frequently. As the country became more mountainous, and the path led through the district of Cazengo, the excellence of the coffee—which grows wild—became more marked, and produced a great impression upon Livingstone. The general fertility of this hilly region is, in fact, indisputable, but in Livingstone's time the arts of cultivation were conspicuous by their absence.

After spending some time at various places in Angola, the party set off again on their eastward march. They were now passing through a district devoid of rivers, and the remarkable scarcity of animal life made the path almost dreary. The herds of graceful antelope, the dark forms of shaggy buffaloes and the sleek-coated elands, so common on the banks of the Zambesi, were absent here. The atmosphere was still and oppressive, and the glare of the sunlight on the evergreen foliage made the occasional shade all the more welcome. For the trees were scattered, and, although grass grew prolificly, scrub and bush were scant.

In the light of Livingstone's later labours on the head-waters of the Congo, and of the recent discoveries by Wissman and Pogge in the basins of the Coango and Kasai, Livingstone's remarks on crossing these two rivers are specially interesting. He learnt through native sources that the Kasai and Coango finally converged—the former receiving the latter—and that the united streams were known as the Zaire, which was an alternative name for the Congo. He also gathered that a large number of streams combined to form the Kasai, a fact which later discoveries have brought out in great prominence: upon the map of Africa the feeders of the Kasai present an almost unique appearance. The large waterfall which he was told interrupted navigation from the sea to the Kasai was, no doubt, that prolonged series of rapids and falls which divides the upper and lower Congo, and which Stanley afterwards named after the Doctor himself. There was no mention, however, on the part of the natives, of the great river which swept round the equator in so wide a semicircle, and of which the Kasai and Coango were simply affluents.

Whenever Livingstone crossed the slave-path, he found the natives suspicious and inclined to be unfriendly. The moment he left it, the reverse obtained: hospitality and extreme civility were the rule. Guides were given without payment being asked, and food was supplied to the strangers as willingly as if they had been bidden guests. In only two cases, and this when on the slave-path, were they required to pay a tribute for passing through the country. Those who remember what Livingstone had to endure in after-years in Central Africa, and the extortions which many who have followed in his tracks have been subjected to, will realise what a boon to the impecunious traveller this freedom from imposts meant.

There was one trait among the African tribes which always struck Livingstone. Very little quarrelling went on among people of the same tribe. At times a good deal of shouting and gesticulation, not to mention swearing, would arise, but the proceedings usually ended in a laugh. He records, however, at this stage of his journey one instance of a "row." An old woman, who was standing looking on at the white man and the strangers, spent nearly the whole of an afternoon in abusing a young man who formed with her one of a gaping group. He stood it like a Stoic for a long time, and then remonstrated with more vigour than civility. In a moment another man sprang at him, shouting, "How dare you curse my 'Mama'?" Then ensued a free fight, of a scuffling and hugging rather than pugilistic character. They finally separated, each going for a weapon to "settle it." Both took very good care, though, not to meet each other when provided with weapons which might make the affair serious. Among themselves the natives cannot bear a grudge for long—at least as far as a frank exhibition of it is concerned.

Early in June, soon after crossing the Kasai, the mountain ridges were left behind, and Livingstone entered on the wide plains which on his westward march he had found flooded. Animal life rapidly increased in quantity and variety, and vegetation assumed a brighter and more luxuriant character. At one time they marched across a wide belt of yellow flowers, at another over an equally broad band of flowers in every shade of blue. Again and again this alternation of colour was repeated. It was while crossing this beautiful plain that the Doctor had his twenty-seventh attack of fever. Indeed, throughout his journey across Africa, he was seldom if ever free from this painful feature of African travel.

On arriving at Lake Dilolo, Livingstone discovered that this comparatively small body of water emptied its waters both into the Zambesi and the Kasai; and that, consequently, it distributed its contents as far as the Indian Ocean on the one side, and the Atlantic on the other. It was through this circumstance that the continental structure of Africa became clear to him. The rivers, in the western portion, flowed from elevated ridges into the centre, and he had learnt from the Arabs that much the same occurred in the eastern portion. But that while one drainage system had a southerly declivity, the other pursued a northerly course. In other words, the two great drains of Central Africa are the Congo and the Zambesi.

In reference to this great central plateau, Livingstone's own words are well worth quoting. "I was thus (at Dilolo) on the watershed or highest point of these two great systems, but still not more than four thousand feet above the level of the sea, and a thousand feet lower than the top of the western ridge we had already crossed; yet, instead of lofty snow-clad mountains appearing to verify the conjectures of the speculative, we had extensive plains, over which one may travel a month without seeing anything higher than an ant-hill or a tree. I was not then aware that any one else had discovered the elevated trough form of the centre of Africa."

This last remark is in reference to Sir Roderick Murchison, who put forward this theory while Livingstone was buried in the depths of the continent. It was on the eastern ridge of this basin-like plateau that the Doctor now hoped to find the healthy district for his much-cherished missionary centre.

Many of the native chiefs were most kind to him. Katema, whose domains were on the Lotembwa, and who had treated Livingstone with great hospitality on the last journey, was now rewarded with a scarlet cloak, ornamented with gold tinsel. When he left Livingstone, he mounted on to the shoulders of an attendant. This was intended to be a dignified mode of quitting his guest; but, as Katema was a large man of stout build, and his attendant but slight in frame, the tenure of his seat was apparently precarious, and the general effect not remote from the ludicrous.

Shinte, again, whose town appears on the map as Kabompo, was another friend. He received some cotton cloth by way of return for his hospitality and goodwill, and was much struck with the advantages of direct trade with the white men of the coast. "These Mambari," he said, referring to the natives who were sent from Bihe by the half-caste traders—"these Mambari cheat us by bringing little pieces only; but the next time you pass I shall send men with you, to trade for me in Loanda."

Another friend in the Balonda country was Manenko,

a female chief. She was unable to meet Livingstone on this return journey, but sent her husband, Sambanza, instead. To cement eternal friendship, that blood-brotherhood — here called "kasendi"—which is so common among the tribes of Central Africa, was consummated; and, as Livingstone gives a graphic description of the ceremony, it will be well to quote his words. The ceremony took place between Sambanza and Pitsane, one of the best of the Doctor's men.

"The hands of the parties are joined; small incisions are made on the clasped hands, on the pits of the stomach of each, and on the right cheeks and foreheads. A small quantity of blood is taken off from these points in both parties by means of a stalk of grass. The blood from one person is put into one pot of native beer, and that of the second into another; each then drinks the other's blood, and they are supposed to become perpetual friends or relations. During the drinking of the beer, some of the party continue beating the ground with short clubs, and utter sentences by way of ratifying the treaty. The men belonging to each then finish the beer. The principals in the performance of 'kasendi' are henceforth considered blood-relations, and are bound to disclose to each other any impending evil." The new-made brothers clench the compact by presenting to each other the most valuable things they have about them.

Malarious fever and native hostility were not the only dangers that Livingstone had to face. The wild animals which abound in the Zambesi basin often proved formidable obstacles in the path. Livingstone, however, never feared the lion much, and in his writings he did his best to dethrone that "lord of the desert" from his place in public estimation. Both the elephant and buffalo he considered more dangerous to the unoffending traveller, and on one occasion in this journey he narrowly escaped from death through the malicious attack of a buffalo.

"As I walked slowly," he says, "after the men, on an extensive plain covered with a great crop of grass which was laid by its own weight, I observed that a solitary buffalo, disturbed by others of my own party, was coming to me at a gallop. I glanced around, but the only tree on the plain was a hundred yards off, and there was no escape elsewhere. I therefore cocked my rifle, with the intention of giving him a steady shot in the forehead, when he should come within three or four yards of me. The thought flashed across my mind, 'What if the gun misses fire?' I placed it at my shoulder as he came on at full speed, and that is tremendous, though generally he is a lumbering-looking animal in his paces. A small bush and bunch of grass fifteen yards off made him swerve a little and exposed his shoulder. I just heard the ball crack there as I fell flat on my face. The pain must have made him renounce his purpose, for he bounded close past me on to the water, where he was found dead. In expressing my thankfulness to God among my men, they were much offended with themselves for not being present to shield me from this danger. The tree near me was a camel-thorn, and reminded me that we had come back to the land of thorns again, for the country we had left is one of evergreens."

This passage is worth quoting for more than the adventure it describes, because we can discern in it no fewer than four of the chief traits of Livingstone's character—four of the leading aspects of his whole life. In the first place, is his coolness in the moment of danger; next, his thankfulness to God and his custom of revealing the existence of a kindly Providence to his men; third, the friendly relations that existed between him and them; and, lastly, the habit of the naturalist which noted everything around him with the eye of discernment. however great or near peril might be.

Later on, when paddling down the Zambesi in a

canoe, he met with another adventure—this time with a female hippopotamus. This unwieldy brute, without giving a moment's warning, struck the canoe with her forehead, sending one-half of it clean out of the water. One of the men was thrown into the river, and the rest jumped in and swam to shore, which luckily for them was quite close. It is usual for travellers by water to keep close to shore in the day-time, as at that time the hippopotami, who are sometimes very savage, frequent the middle of the stream. By night, when these brutes approach the banks, travellers withdraw to the middle. It was probably on account of knowing this that the charge of the hippopotamus was all the more surprising to Livingstone and his men.

On arriving in the Barotse country, of which many of his men were natives, there were great rejoicings—marred here and there by the discovery of the fickleness of their wives. These women appear to have considered an absence of two years on the part of their husbands quite sufficient to warrant their re-marriage. Livingstone has told us that "Mashauana's wife, who had borne him two children, was among the number. He wished to appear not to feel it much, saying, 'Why, wives are as plentiful as grass, and I can get another; she may go.' But he would add, 'If I had that fellow, I would open his ears for him.' As most of them had more wives than one, I tried to console them by saying that they had still more than I had, and that they had enough yet; but they felt the reflection to be galling, that while they were toiling another had been devouring their corn."

In September 1855 they marched into Sesheke, and Livingstone found some goods and letters, which had been lying there for twelve months, awaiting his return. Not only had nothing been taken, but a hut had been built over them for protection from the weather. Similarly, on reaching Linyanti he found everything

LIVINGSTONE'S BOAT OVERTURNED BY A HIPPOPOTAMUS.

just as he had left it. This was a striking example of honesty, for the Makololo were feared through a wide region for their marauding spirit and fondness for raiding among their neighbours' cattle.

The return of the travellers was a time of great rejoicing. All the wonderful things which the Makololo had seen and met with were rehearsed a hundred times to an audience whose appreciation never waned, and whose appetite seemed only whetted by the tales of the marvellous adventures their kinsmen had gone through. The presents that the Portuguese officials and merchants had sent to Sekeletu were duly delivered; and "on Sunday," says Livingstone, "when Sekeletu made his appearance at church in his uniform, it attracted more attention than the sermon."

Livingstone's unvarying kindness to his men, and the hospitable nature of the treatment the Portuguese had extended to his followers, were not forgotten. They spoke so well of their leader, both in public and in private, that he soon had plenty of volunteers clamouring for him to lead them down the Zambesi to the sea. And what pleased him more was the fact that the Makololo seemed keenly alive to the benefit of trading direct with Loanda, and at once set about preparing for another expedition thither. Although this first trip on their own account was not altogether successful, it was owing to their inexperience in trade rather than any physical obstacles presented by the journey. And, at any rate, there seemed every probability of legitimate trade ousting that nefarious traffic which had begun in slaves.

On the 3rd of November, 1855, Livingstone left Linyanti and resumed his long march across Africa. Sekeletu and a large number of followers accompanied him for some distance, and then bade him an affectionate farewell. Livingstone's sojourn among the Makololo had been marked with conspicuous success;

for, although the actual conversions were few, the influence of the Gospel of peace had been shed about their lives, and had in many cases touched their hearts. The Doctor was regarded with the deepest respect, and his constant and continual revelation of the character of Christ and the benefits of Christianity had found many attentive listeners. His labours had been rewarded with a well-defined result, and he left the people better than he had found them. Livingstone always believed that, if the seed were only faithfully sown, it could not fail to ripen in some degree. He considered it was really more efficacious to preach the Gospel and exhibit the consistency of a Christian life to large numbers of people, and then allow it to slowly mature through the independent interest and action of the people themselves, than to settle permanently in one spot, and by a life-long ministry among comparatively few render those few dependent on the missionary's personal efforts, and blind to the active agency which was latent in themselves. His views on this question were directed by a wonderful knowledge of the native character, and they would have received a more universal support and approval had those who followed in his track been gifted with his own perspicuity of vision and patient nobility of character.

A day or so after parting from Sekeletu, Livingstone came in sight of the great falls of the Zambesi, and which were known to the natives as "Mosi-oa-tunya" —" smoke does sound there." The noble river, a mile in width, sweeps down a broad and wooded valley, which, sloping gently back from the banks, culminates in swelling hills some three or four hundred feet in height. Trees of many kinds, from the massive baobab to the slender palm, grow in clumps or singly upon this grassy slope. From the bosom of the river arise palm-fostering islands, and on its banks the silver cedar spreads its branches, the clustering fruit of the wild date-palm gleams like gold, and the scarlet-fruited cypress lifts its dark head above the surrounding foliage. The vegetation is tropical, but the scene has a repose which is rare indeed in a region where all forms of life are exuberant and aggressive.

These are some of the beauties of the most remarkable scene in the Zambesi basin. But the traveller passes them by almost unheeded; for right in front of him, and riveting his gaze, there rise into the heavens five lofty columns of vapour, for all the world like smoke. These five great towers of Nature's building curl and bend to the faintest breeze, and yet never cease to soar till they are dissipated in the rarified atmosphere of greater elevation, or, mingling with the clouds of a spent storm, are lost from view. They are the sentinels over the most wonderful sight Nature has prepared for man in Africa—a physical phenomenon of a pre-eminence which induced Livingstone to baptize them with a name of equal pre-eminence in his own country, and reveal to an astounded world that unrivalled plunge of waters as the Victoria Falls.

Livingstone cautiously paddled to an island in midstream and on the very brink of the falls, and this is what met his view: " Creeping with awe to the verge, I peered down into a large rent which had been made from bank to bank of the broad Zambesi. . . . In looking down into the fissure on the right of the island, one sees nothing but a dense white cloud, which, at the time we visited the spot, had two bright rainbows on it. From this cloud rushed up a great jet of vapour exactly like steam, and it mounted two or three hundred feet high; there, condensing, it changed its hue to that of dark smoke, and came back in a constant shower. . . . On the left of the island we see the water at the bottom, a white rolling mass moving away to the prolongation of the fissure, which branches off near the left bank of the river. . . . The entire falls are

THE VICTORIA FALLS, ZAMBESI RIVER.

simply a crack made in a hard basaltic rock from the right to the left bank of the Zambesi, and then prolonged from the left bank away through thirty or forty miles of hills. . . . The walls of this gigantic crack are perpendicular, and composed of one homogeneous mass of rock."

These falls are about three hundred feet high and eighteen hundred yards in width. The fissure into which they plunge is so narrow as to be invisible till the verge is reached.

Livingstone was so impressed with this splendid creation that he retraced his steps and persuaded Sekeletu to visit the falls with him. The effect on the native mind was one of intense awe.

The discovery of the falls, taken in conjunction with many other facts known to him, led Livingstone to conclude that in earlier times a large portion of Central Africa had been one vast series of lakes, and that these lakes had disappeared in the fissures which the forces of upheaval had created in the elevated ridges which rim the central basin. As instances of similar outlets, the Congo and the Orange Rivers, flowing through deep and narrow gorges on reaching the external ridge, may be cited. In passing over the apex of the ridge in the neighbourhood of the Zambesi, Livingstone found it five hundred feet in height, and these eastern highlands more healthy than those he had already discovered in the west. There was, moreover, the additional advantage of a highway for civilizing and commercial purposes in the great Zambesi River. He had therefore at last come to a region in which he might look with some certainty of success for a district entirely suitable to Europeans, and capable of being utilized as a great missionary settlement and centre.

And at this stage of the journey the natives were both hospitable and amenable to influence. "All," he says, "expressed great satisfaction on hearing my

LIVINGSTONE'S PARTY ATTACKED BY BUFFALOES.

message, as I directed their attention to Jesus as their Saviour, whose word is, 'Peace on earth and good will to men.' They called out, 'We are tired of flight; give us rest and sleep.'" Later on, however, the natives, mistaking him for a half-caste Portuguese, showed a good deal of hostility, and Livingstone very narrowly escaped with his life from the people of Mpende, who dwelt near the confluence of the Loangwa and Zambesi.

The country through which they were passing was exceedingly beautiful. At first furrowed by wide fertile glens, and afterwards opening out into a luxuriant plain, abounding with animal life and vegetation, and possessing the inestimable advantage of salubrity, the Doctor felt that he had at last reached the land of promise for the missionary cause. Many of the hills were of pure white marble, and pink marble formed the bed of more than one of the contributory streams. Upon the plains enormous herds of zebras, buffaloes, and elephants grazed between the patches of dense forest which here and there studded the grassy level. Through this country the Zambesi rolled down toward the coast at the rate of about four miles an hour, while flocks of water-fowl swarmed upon its banks or took their flight across its waters.

So plentiful was game, that the leading men had frequently to shout to the elephants or buffaloes which stood in their path. Sometimes an elephant would charge right through the little party; at another time it would be a buffalo. Upon one occasion several buffaloes suddenly charged at full gallop into their midst, one of them tossing a Makololo high into the air. Wonderful to relate, he fell upon the ground uninjured! He had been carried some distance on the horns of the buffalo, and then tossed; yet not only was no bone broken, but even the skin was uninjured. The man was carefully "shampooed"—or, to use a phrase more in vogue just now, *massaged*—and in a few days was actively engaged in hunting buffaloes for food.

In March Livingstone arrived at Tete, the furthest outpost of the Portuguese, and was most kindly received by the governor. Fever again prostrated him, and it was not till the end of April that he could set out once more for Quilimane. He left his Makololo men at Tete. Nearly three years elapsed before he rejoined them, but he had promised to return and take them home, and, believing in him implicitly, they had remained.

Livingstone went from Tete to Sena, and, though suffering greatly from fever, he pushed on as soon as he could move, and passing the important affluence of the Shiré River finally reached Quilimane, and gazed on the gleaming waters of the Indian Ocean on the 20th of May, 1856. "Here," he wrote, "I was received into the house of Colonel Nunes, one of the best men in the country. . . . One of the discoveries I have made is that there are vast numbers of good people in the world, and I do most devoutly tender my unfeigned thanks to that Gracious One who mercifully watched over me in every position, and influenced the hearts of both black and white to regard me with favour."

AFRICAN COCKATOOS.

CHAPTER V.

HOME.

AFTER waiting six weeks on the "great mudbank, surrounded by extensive swamps and ricegrounds," which forms the site of Quilimane, Livingstone embarked in a British gun-boat for the Mauritius. Here he experienced the same generous hospitality which had been extended to him at Quilimane, and when he sailed in November for England it was with recuperated strength and some of his old sturdy Scotch vigour. After narrowly escaping shipwreck in the Mediterranean, he finally reached England on the 9th of December, 1856.

The welcome that awaited him partook of a national character, for from end to end of Great Britain congratulations and honours came pouring in upon him, and the whole country rang with his name and his achievements in Africa. In the midst of much to cause thankfulness and joy, there was a sorrow which he felt most keenly. Beside the hearth of his cottage home at Blantyre stood his father's empty chair. While Livingstone was on his homeward journey, the father to whom he had longed to tell his wonderful experiences and who had looked so eagerly for his return, crowned an upright life by dying the death of a righteous man.

On the other hand, the meeting of the long-separated husband and wife was a source of unmixed happiness. These had been trying years for Mrs. Livingstone, who had reared her family on straitened means, and with a heart which had never been free from anxiety since she left her husband at Capetown. Henceforth, as it seemed then, they were never to be separated again. Mary Livingstone accompanied her husband when he returned to Africa, and, though once more separated from him on account of her ill-health, she had the unspeakable satisfaction of rejoining him when in Nyassaland, and being comforted by his strong faith and deep affection when she lay at Shupanga on her death-bed.

But we anticipate. The Royal Geographical Society of course called a meeting to greet their distinguished medallist. Sir Roderick Murchison, with whom Livingstone had been in constant correspondence, presided, and among those present were three old friends of the early Bakwain days—Oswell, Steele, and Vardon. The eleven thousand miles which Livingstone had travelled through Africa, "in sickness and in health," were made the subject of great congratulations, and the nobility of the Doctor's character received a full and sympathetic acknowledgment. An unusually distinguished assembly accorded the intrepid traveller—the Christian missionary—the heartiest greeting and most unstinted approval.

Following on the meeting of the Geographical Society came that of the London Missionary Society. The reception he received was equally warm and cordial, although Livingstone had made up his mind to sever his connection with the Society. To understand the reason for this we must go back a little.

When Livingstone emerged from the dense obscurity

of the interior of Africa and came in touch with the civilized world at Quilimane, he received a letter from the Society to the effect that "they were restricted in their power of aiding plans connected only remotely with the spread of the Gospel, and that the financial circumstances of the Society were not such as to afford any ground of hope that it would be in a position, within any definite period, to enter upon untried, remote, and difficult fields of labour." Livingstone took, as any other man for the matter of that would have taken, this to be throwing a "wet blanket" upon his enthusiasm, and a hint that no support could be looked for in further explorations of a similar nature. The Society appeared desirous of shelving the Doctor's plans; so he did what he considered best under the circumstances, and shelved the Society. Referring to this letter in his work, Livingstone said, "This has been explained since as an effusion caused by temporary financial depression; but, feeling perfect confidence in my Makololo friends, I was determined to return and trust to their generosity. The old love of independence, which I had so strongly before joining the Society, again returned." In other words, the connection between him and the London Missionary Society was to cease.

At the public reception given by the Society to Livingstone, nothing but kindly things were said, and Lord Shaftesbury, who presided, paid a well-deserved tribute to the wife of the great explorer. "That lady was born," said he, "with one distinguished name, which she changed for another. She was born a Moffat, and she became a Livingstone." The public is better informed now than it was then, or Lord Shaftesbury would have had no need to say one word more in the praise of the dutiful daughter of Robert Moffat, and the courageous wife of David Livingstone.

A month later, he was beginning his first book—that

volume which, under the title of "Missionary Travels," was destined to win a world-wide reputation as a singularly complete and able history of his labours and travels in Africa. The broad view which he took of his duty as a missionary, and the conscientiousness with which he acted up to it on every occasion, are remarkably conspicuous in the pages of that most interesting work. Many subjects are treated in it, and all with scientific fidelity to fact. There is no attempt at ornate diction, and no trace of exaggeration. Those "travellers' tales" of daring and adventure, which are so frequent in works of a similar nature, are not to be found there. When a remarkable discovery or a real danger is noted, the language employed is so calm that a casual reader might imagine the writer indifferent to their importance. Here we find a careful description of some geographical fact, and there one of a commercial opportunity. Anthropology, botany, geology, astronomy, medicine, commerce, sociology, statistics, folk-lore, philology, and other important branches of universal knowledge are all represented. Such examples of them as he found are described with the careful exactness of the student, and discussed with a breadth of view peculiar to the philosopher. And yet through all this intricate fabric of fact—through warp and woof—there runs the golden thread which directed and animated all his efforts, and hallowed the labours of his life. His intense desire to benefit Africa and the African—to rid the one of the blot with which slavery had darkened it, and to bring to the other the abiding benefits of the Gospel of peace and good will—glows through all the notes of the naturalist, and illumines the gloomiest page in which the degradation of the native races is recorded. The book is a mirror of the scenes and people he encountered, and an unintentional monument to his own noble devotion to a self-imposed duty.

Financially, too, the book was a success. Published

at a guinea, the first edition of twelve thousand was at once exhausted. Eminent specialists vied with the Press in giving it unbounded approval. The practical world of commerce was as much delighted as the scientific circles or the Christian churches. Possibilities hitherto undreamed of—possibilities for financial as well as philanthropic schemes—were revealed when Livingstone gave this record of his missionary travels to the reading world.

On all sides and by every one he was sought At Glasgow, Dublin, Edinburgh, Oxford, Cambridge, Hamilton, and his own native Blantyre, he gave addresses, which were listened to with equal interest by the learned and the unlearned, the old and the young. Honorary degrees were conferred on him by Oxford, Cambridge, and Glasgow. He was elected to the Royal Society on the proposal of a distinguished fellow "on behalf of the Queen." The freedom of the City of London, of Glasgow, of Edinburgh, and other cities was bestowed on him. The medals of the French Geographical Society and the Society of Arts were awarded him, and in person he received the gold medal of the Royal Geographical Society. He was elected to the corresponding membership of all the chief geographical societies of the world, and his own College of Physicians and Surgeons at Glasgow welcomed him to the rare privilege of an "Honorary Fellowship."

A list of some of the many distinctions which were showered upon this "plain, single-minded man, somewhat attenuated by years of toil, and with a face tinged by the sun of Africa," should not be closed without a reference to his visit to Windsor. The Queen, who never shows to more advantage than when honouring some illustrious subject by that graceful courtesy for which she herself is so distinguished, sent for Livingstone. In the course of the interview she asked many thoughtful, searching questions, and received replies which amused as well as informed. Here is one. Livingstone told her that the African chiefs were always asking him if his chief were rich, and when answered in the affirmative, would ask, "How many cows has she?" With this method of gauging her wealth, the Queen was highly amused.

This quiet man from the wilds of Africa was made, against his will, the "lion of the season." Mobbed in Regent Street; pointedly referred to in church by an indiscreet clergyman who had noticed him, and consequently rushed at by the congregation—even across the pews—as soon as the last "Amen" and long before decency allowed them; overwhelmed with invitations to banquets and the dinner-tables of the influential and wealthy; written to by a legion of inquisitive rather than inquiring persons; called on and accosted by "somebodies" and "nobodies" with equal impropriety—Livingstone found much of his life in London more lively than pleasant. Indeed, during a period of his stay in England, he lived in the suburbs and the country rather than risk the inconvenient if kindly attentions that were paid to him. Not that he was insensible to the feeling which was exhibited towards him, but that he desired for himself a little of the consideration which he was always ready to accord to others.

Livingstone's views on Africa and the work to be done in its vast equatorial regions were emphatic. He placed the slave tade, openly introduced by the Arabs and bolstered up by the Portuguese, at the head of the abuses to be swept away. As long as it was permitted to exist, he saw plainly that no real advance could be made in the civilization and conversion of the native races. The distrust which it bred in the native mind, and the hostility of the traders to those who would suppress it, rendered the journeys of the missionary perilous and his labours futile. That legitimate trade which the introduction of commerce would provide was, in Livingstone's opinion, the most potent weapon with which to lay this hideous spectre. It appealed directly to the self-interests of the natives, and revealed to them the value of labour. While the resources of fertile Central Africa were undeveloped, the value of this labour was obscured; but directly it was perceived that by cultivating the soil, producing raw material, and conveying it to centres of trade an enormous increase in prosperity would ensue, the natives—who were keenly alive to the main chance—would spontaneously desert the traffic in blood and flesh, and utilize their captives in war, or those of their own tribes whom they sold, for the more remunerative purposes of agriculture and commerce. The slave trade, by emptying the country of this labour material, was practically rendering such a state of things impossible, and shutting up the interior in all its hopeless degradation and helplessness. By abolishing the slave trade, therefore, legitimate commerce and the introduction of the ways and means of civilization were made as probable as they were possible; and, hand in hand with civilization, the teachings of the Christian missionary would dignify labour, inculcate peace, secure honesty, and generally elevate the whole of the population.

With the slave trade but little was possible; the slave trade suppressed, all things would seem easy.

This and much more were the texts of every speech that Livingstone made in England. Referring to his approaching departure, he said in one of his speeches at Cambridge: "For my own part, I intend to go out as a missionary, and hope boldly, but with civility, to state the truth of Christianity, and my belief that those who do not possess it are in error. My object in Africa is not only the elevation of man, but that the country might be so opened that man might see the need of his soul's salvation."

Upon another occasion, when writing to one who thought there was too much "geography" and not enough "grace" in his book, he said: "My views of what is *missionary* are not so contracted as those whose ideal is a dumpy sort of man with a Bible under his arm. I have laboured in bricks and mortar, at the forge and carpenter's bench, as well as in preaching and medical practice. I feel that 'I am not my own.' I am serving Christ when shooting a buffalo for my men, or taking an astronomical observation, or writing to one of His children who forget, during the little moment of penning a note, that charity which is eulogized as 'thinking no evil.'"

In fact, as Livingstone says more than once in his book, the leading influence of his life and the most powerful motive to all his actions are contained in these words: "The end of the geographical feat is but the beginning of the missionary enterprise."

Notwithstanding the excellent reasons which he adduced to the contrary, there were not wanting those who thought he had submerged the missionary in the explorer. His firm but courteous refusal to act any longer as an agent of the London Missionary Society—for taking which step he said afterwards, "I never felt a single pang"—placed him in a singularly independent position when such an objection was raised, and gave him a practical argument which was hard to confute: "Knowing that some persons do believe that opening up a new country to the sympathies of Christendom was not a proper work for an agent of a missionary society to engage in, I now refrain from taking any salary from the Society with which I was connected, so no pecuniary loss is sustained by any one."

Many of the Portuguese—especially those materially interested—were furious with Livingstone for his exposure of their support of the slave trade, and for pointing out how opposed their policy was to the development of commerce. Livingstone, however, made out too good a case for even the " special pleaders " of that nation's colonial policy. The prevalence of barbarism in Portuguese settlements, the shadowy authority of the officials over even the districts which were nearest to the coast, the exclusion of commerce other than the nefarious system they monopolized, the obstructive tariff imposed at the two or three ports which they possessed, their ignorance of the country behind the maritime belt, and their unpleasant relations with such tribes as adjoined them, were points which one and all Livingstone hit right on the head and drove home with convincing force.

The national feeling, the opinion of the authorities, and the work and writings of Livingstone himself could have but one conclusion. In February 1858, he was appointed British consul for East Africa and the districts of the interior, and at the same time offered the leadership of an expedition for the exploration of Central and Eastern Africa.

The object of the expedition was not merely geographical. The officers in charge were to encourage by example and precept the cultivation of such industries as would enable the natives to embark on a reciprocal trade with Great Britain; to inquire into the extent and utility of such resources as were at hand and capable of being immediately realised; and, above all, to influence the minds of the natives by " an example of consistent moral conduct," to treat them kindly and minister to their bodily comfort, to teach them the simple arts of manufacture, to instruct them in the broad virtues of the Christian faith, and to insist—in season and, if necessary, out of season—on the benefits of their living together in unity, peace, and goodwill.

With such an object, there was little doubt that Livingstone would gladly take over the control of the Zambesi expedition. As consul his position with regard to the Portuguese was assured, for he came to the task with the credentials of the British Government; and the position itself enabled him to make more extended investigations, and placed at his disposal a greater degree of power. His own views of the means by which the much-to-be desired end was to be accomplished were ably summed up in his instructions to the officers of the expedition, a few words from which may be quoted here.

"We come among them (the natives) as members of a superior race, and servants of a government that desires to elevate the more degraded portions of the human family. We are adherents of a benign, holy religion, and may by consistent conduct, and wise, patient efforts, become the harbingers of peace to a hitherto distracted and trodden-down race."

Thus it is very evident that Livingstone had no idea of merging the missionary in the explorer to the immolation of the former, but that he was about to exemplify in his own person a dual office for the first time exhibited to the world—that of the Consul-Missionary.

IN CAMP.

CHAPTER VI.

IN THE ZAMBESI COUNTRY.

ON the 10th of March, 1858, the Zambesi Expedition left England, and, sailing *viâ* the Cape of Good Hope, arrived off the mouths of the great river in the following May.

The short stay that was made at Capetown *en route* proved an eventful one to Livingstone. It was considered better that his wife, who was in poor health and suffered much from fever symptoms, should remain for a while with her parents, who were then at Capetown, and rejoin her husband at a later date. This was a disappointment to the latter as deep as it was unexpected, and, although he does not refer specially to it in his published journals, in letters to friends he characterizes the separation as "a great trial."

There was, however, some compensation prepared for him in the enthusiastic reception he was accorded by the people of Capetown and the authorities of the Colony. It will be remembered that when last at Capetown, in 1852, he was regarded with considerable disfavour, owing to the reports which the Boers had brought to the Colony. Now, however, the tables were turned, and the man whom the people of Capetown delighted to specially honour was Livingstone. At a great and enthusiastic public meeting, the governor, Sir George Grey, presented him with the sum of eight hundred guineas, enclosed in a silver casket, which had been raised by public subscription as a testimonial to the value of the services he had performed—which services, it was seen, would largely benefit Africa as a whole, and Cape Colony in particular.

Among the members of the expedition were Charles Livingstone, the brother of the Doctor, who had returned from clerical work in America on purpose to assist him in his further explorations; and Dr. (now Sir) John Kirk, who was to be the naturalist and physician of the expedition, and subsequently for many years our highly-esteemed consul at Zanzibar. The party brought with them, packed in sections, a small steam-launch for use on the Zambesi, and which was named *Ma-Robert* after his wife, who had been given that name by the Bakwains in accordance with their custom of naming the mother (Ma) after her first-born.

The delta of the Zambesi is of considerable extent, its coast-side, from the Quilimane branch on the north to the Luabo on the south, being some eighty miles in length. The Quilimane channel, however, is now choked by vegetation, and consequently dry during the greater part of the year. The Luabo is the chief mouth, and the river is navigable inland without a single break for nearly three hundred miles—to the Portuguese settlement of Tete. A few miles above the apex of the delta the river receives the Shiré, which is the overflow of the important Nyassa Lake. The Zambesi is the great drain of the pastoral belt of South Africa, and its basin has an area of some eight hundred thousand square miles—or, in other words, is more than four times the size of France. The importance of the river and its fertile basin is great, and the recent labours of the English and Scotch in various parts of the country which lie within its drainage system have revealed with emphasis the value of the discoveries and pioneering of Livingstone a generation ago.

The shores of the delta are low, closely embraced by a mangrove jungle, and pierced on all sides by those stagnant lagoons which the dense and spreading roots of the mangrove invariably create or foster. For some twenty miles inland from the Kongone mouth, up which the *Ma-Robert* ultimately steamed, the mangrove jungle was found to be very dense; and Livingstone, making every effort to reach a more healthy region, passed through a belt of wide level plains of rich alluvial soil, covered with grass which grew to a height of over ten feet. The natives of this belt of country live in houses raised on piles above the reach of flood, and entered by ladders. The fertility of the soil is indisputable, and is capable of providing Europe with an enormous amount of sugar and rice, for the cultivation of which its low level and moist nature render it admirably adapted. From within twenty miles of the sea to the head of the delta this region of fertile plains extends, and, although the climate is by no means suitable for the European, a vast industry might have arisen here, had not the folly and greed of the Portuguese, by indulging in the slave trade, emptied the country of the needful labour.

At Shupanga, the elevation of the country is somewhat greater, and as a consequence the climate a trifle less malignant. From here, however, to Sena, Livingstone found the Portuguese at war with the natives, and travelling became dangerous as well as difficult. The tribes on the southern bank were of Zulu race, and the Portuguese paid them an annual tribute for the right of living and trading in their country. The tribes on the north were of inferior physique and character, and upon these the Portuguese preyed so unceasingly, that the native spirit was goaded beyond sufferance, and often broke out in what can hardly be called rebellion. The system or no-system of colonization which was pursued was proving somewhat expensive, for at the time Livingstone wrote the province of Mozambique was a heavy charge upon the Home Government, and yielded nothing in return.

Passing Sena—which is built on the level bank of the Zambesi, and has a background of moderate hills and a look-out across the river upon a lofty and picturesque range—the Doctor pressed forward to Tete. Here he was received by the Makololo—whom he had left there nearly three years before—with the greatest affection and enthusiasm. Some of them had died, but the survivors philosophically remarked that "men die in any country." While Livingstone was in England, the Portuguese Government had informed the English authorities that they had sent orders to support these Makololo until the Doctor should return to them. Acting on this information, Livingstone had not returned as soon as he had intended. On arrival at Tete, however, he found that not only had the Portuguese Government omitted to forward the necessary intimation of their good intentions—in order to carry them into effect—but that even the pay of the officials of the province was several years in arrear! Little likely were the Makololo to receive official countenance and support when the maintenance of the officials themselves depended on their own personal efforts in the way of slave-trading and other methods of gain more or less legitimate. As it happened, however, the personal generosity of the Governor had materially assisted the Makololo in their endeavour to support themselves.

Tete stands upon some low ridges on the right bank of the Zambesi, and in Livingstone's time it was surrounded by a stone and mud wall, the huts of the natives being outside this line of defence. The Doctor found many tons of indigo growing, not only in the vicinity, but even in the streets of the town. Indeed, the indigo plant was the chief weed of the place, and regarded as such a nuisance that it was annually burned off, exactly in the same way as the natives burned off the tall jungle grass. This one fact is a good illustration of the neglect of the Portuguese to avail themselves of the natural resources of the country in which they had settled.

In spite of this, Tete was a place of some importance, owing to its being the furthest inland settlement of the Portuguese. As a natural consequence, the Europeans of Tete were slave traders and the possessors as well as the vendors of numerous slaves. Not infrequently they enriched themselves by trading in ivory and gold-dust; but gradually the lucrativeness of that traffic in human beings, called with grim humour "black ivory," or "ebony," drew them away from the stable pursuit of agriculture to a feverish quest after slaves. The result is evidenced in the state of Tete to-day. The fertile fields, no longer cultivated, have returned to their former jungle condition; and, having neither men to work nor fight for them, the Portuguese Government has abandoned the town, which is fast lapsing to decay.

A short distance above Tete, the navigation of the Zambesi is interrupted by the Kebrabasa rapids. Livingstone and Kirk examined these falls with the greatest care no less than three times, and they came to the conclusion that, while impossible of navigation at ordinary times, it might be possible to do so at the flood season, when the river rose a great height in the rocky cañon which formed its bed, and buried the rocks and rapids below. But the force of the stream at this time was too great for the *Ma-Robert* to stem, and accordingly Livingstone sent a report back to the

Government, pointing out the difficulties, and asking for a more powerful steamer.

In the meanwhile, he turned his attention to the Shiré. Of this river the Portuguese could tell him nothing but what was erroneous. An expedition, it was said, had attempted to ascend it in former years, but the impenetrable mass of aquatic vegetation had made advance impossible. Moreover, the Manganja, who dwelt on its banks, were regarded as savages of the most bloodthirsty type. "Our government," said one commandant, "has sent us orders to assist and protect you, but you go where we dare not follow, and how can we protect you?" As a matter of fact, both Livingstone and Kirk were reported as having been killed very shortly after their departure!

Upon entering the Shiré, in January 1859, a good deal of duckweed was met with, but never in sufficient mass to stem the progress of canoes or boats, and after a few miles it almost disappeared. The natives, however, were very much in evidence, and at first assumed an attitude of marked hostility. But on being told that the white men were English, and that statement receiving some support from the entirely novel boat in which they travelled, the natives became friendly, and Tingane, a notorious chief, and a known foe to the Portuguese, extended his hospitality and protection toward them.

A passage occurs in Livingstone's book, "The Zambesi and its Tributaries," which may be quoted at this point, as showing the method adopted by him on going among these savage tribes as a perfect stranger.

"In commencing intercourse with any people we almost always referred to the English detestation of slavery. Most of them already possess some information respecting the efforts made by the English at sea to suppress the slave trade; and our work being to induce them to raise and sell cotton, instead of capturing and selling their fellow-men, our errand appears quite natural; and as they all have clear ideas of their own self-interest and are keen traders, the reasonableness of the proposal is at once admitted; and as a belief in a Supreme Being, the Maker and Ruler of all things, and in the continued existence of departed spirits, is universal, it becomes quite appropriate to explain that we possess a Book containing a revelation of the will of Him, to whom in their natural state they recognise no relationship."

Throughout the most laborious journeys, in the days of pain and disease, as well as those of vigour and health, Livingstone made a regular practice of reading the Bible to his native followers, and explaining to them the blessings of that Universal Fatherhood which regards all men as brothers. To the revelation of such a life as that of the Great Physician they would listen with the amazement of children, and be lost in wonder at Him who laid down His life for enemies and friends alike. For it is not the ruling idea of Christianity which is a stumbling-block to the native; it is his inability, after ages of moral darkness, to entirely eschew the evil and cleave to the good. Livingstone, in his compassion, made allowances for this; and those who have taken up his work do well to remember it. Is the "civilized" Christian so consistent that he can afford to cast a stone at the stark Heathen?

A hundred miles "as the crow flies" from the confluence of the Shiré and Zambesi—or, if the meanderings of the river are taken into account, some two hundred miles from that point—further navigation was prevented by the lowest of those large cataracts which, from gratitude and with appropriateness, Livingstone afterwards called the Murchison Cataracts. As the natives were too suspicious—they kept watch over the little party night and day—for

LIVINGSTONE READING THE BIBLE TO THE NATIVES.

it to be prudent to advance along the bank, the Doctor sent friendly messages to the neighbouring chiefs, with a view to future relations, and returned to Tete.

A month later, he and Kirk again arrived at the foot of the falls, and, travelling in a north-easterly direction across country, they came to the shores of Lake Shirwa on the 18th of April, 1859. This lake had never been heard of before, and consequently it was a genuine, an absolute discovery. Some seventy miles in length and twenty in breadth, Lake Shirwa lies amid beautiful scenery. The lofty ridge of Zomba, nine thousand feet in height, which separates the lake from the Shiré, is its western boundary; and on the east rises the Malanje chain, a range of equal magnitude. But the importance of this discovery was enhanced tenfold when Livingstone learnt from the natives around its shores that there was another lake to the north, only separated from the Shirwa by a narrow belt of land, and compared with which the Shirwa "was nothing in size."

The Doctor did not hasten forward to this new lake, as he would have done had he been a mere explorer; but, considering that the gaining of the natives' confidence was of more value than exploration, he returned slowly to the Shiré, making friends as he went, and finally reached Tete in safety.

From here Livingstone and Dr. Kirk steamed down to the mouth of the Kongone, in anticipation of meeting a man-of-war, which it had been arranged should bring them provisions. This particular vessel failed to make its appearance; but by good fortune another arrived, and from it they were enabled to re-victual. Before returning to Tete, the *Ma-Robert* was hauled up on land and her bottom, which was degenerating with marked rapidity into the condition of a sieve, repaired with a deal of labour and considerable expenditure of time. The boat had proved a failure for many reasons; and if her builder had arrived on the

Zambesi at the time the *Asthmatic*—as the members of the expedition called her—was snorting her laborious way from Kongone to Tete, his reception at the hands of her crew would probably have been even warmer than that which the climate accorded. Slow speed, leaky decks, badly-fitted compartments—so that the water filtered through the sides and wetted everything, even the beds and bedding—were among the chief faults of the *Ma-Robert*. The disappointment was great, for much had been expected, especially as the builder had assured them that extra good material and workmanship had been put into the launch, owing to his "love for the work" which the *Ma-Robert* was so materially to assist!

In August the Shiré was ascended for the third time. The people on this occasion were in nearly every case peaceably inclined, and Livingstone had ample opportunity to study their customs and inquire into their beliefs. It was here he first met with the *pelele* contrivance, which in the opinion of the native women so greatly adorns them. When told it was ugly, they replied much as their European sisters might—" Really ! It is the fashion." The pelele consists of a ring so inserted in the upper lip as to draw it out in a horizontal line at least two inches beyond the nose. The ring may be of metal or ivory, and is inserted at an early age.

These Manganja were found to believe in a Supreme Being, and also in a future state. " We live," said one old chief, " only a few days here, but we live again after death. We do not know where, or in what condition, or with what companions, for the dead never return to tell us. Sometimes the dead do come back and appear to us in dreams; but they never speak nor tell us where they have gone, nor how they fare."

Livingstone was so interested in these people that, writing to Mr. James Young, his old college friend, he said, " I am tired of discovery when no fruit follows," and went on to describe the amount of toil which the *Ma-Robert* entailed on them, wasting time which might have been employed in delivering the message to the people. The quantity of fuel she consumed was enormous, and even with her furnace full but little speed was attained.

On the 16th of September, 1859, the great Lake Nyassa was discovered. This lake is more than three hundred miles in length, and about forty miles in width. It fills a long trench, which is some six hundred feet deep below the level of the lake, and is walled in on the east by a lofty range of mountains, reaching in the north-east an elevation of ten thousand feet. The lake was found to be right in the track of a great inland trade. From the country of Katanga and Cazembe, from those densely-peopled districts lying west of the Nyassa, came Arab caravans bringing the produce of the country—ivory, malachite, copper ornaments, and too often, even then, gangs of slaves—down to the east coast, to the ports of the Portuguese and the Arabs, to Iboe, Mozambique, and Kilwa.

Livingstone saw clearly that if he could establish a steamer upon this lake, and buy the ivory from the natives with European goods, he would at once strike a deadly blow at the slave trade. The overland journey to the coast was so long and laborious that it only paid the Arabs to bring slaves from far Katanga and Lunda when they could utilize them for carrying the ivory. The presence of this steamer would largely affect the interior trade, because the traders were not allowed by the natives to pass by the northern end of the Nyassa; so that with water communication from end to end of the lake, and, excepting the one break of sixty miles at the Murchison Cataracts, thence *viâ* the Shiré and Zambesi to the sea, a comparatively small number of men and but two or three boats would be sufficient to hold the nefarious traffic in check. This able method of coping with the difficulties of the question was originated, and for a long time cherished, by Livingstone. He saw the

> "Argosies of magic sails,
> Pilots of the purple twilight, dropping down with costly bales,"

from that new-found Cathay, reaching to the world of Europe and the shores of his beloved Britain. The trade which devastated the country and blunted the best feelings of the people, which made labour and commerce impossible, and man

> "Neither brute nor human,
> But a ghoul,"

—this trade was to be swept away, the people taught to obtain what they wanted by exchanging the fruit of their own industry, humanized by peaceful labour and Christianized by sowers of the Gospel seed, life made pleasant and sacred as well as safe, homes provided by the salubrious slopes of the mountains encircling Nyassa for Europeans who could work with their own hands while "their tongues were not dumb"—this was the vision which arose before Livingstone's eyes as they looked across the gleaming lake and rested on the unbroken horizon, and it was the desire to bring about its fulfilment that led him back to the Zambesi and in touch once more with those friends in far-off England who were best able to assist him to this end.

He was at this period most sanguine of a great success, and there can be no doubt that he would have achieved something like it had not the attitude of the Portuguese and the villainies of the slave traders conspired to undo what he had already begun to do. He could no longer be in doubt as to the real feelings of the majority of the officials in East Africa; for although the Home Government continued to send out orders for his support, these orders were neglected and ignored. It became only too evident to these "official" gentry that Livingstone meant no half-measures, but the out-and-out eradication of the slave trade. And as this would involve the financial ruin of the governors, deputy-governors, commandants, and a host of small fry who were more or less openly engaged in the profitable "black ivory" trade, it became the object of the Portuguese on the Zambesi to put every difficulty in Livingstone's way, to blacken his character and read his motives backward, with all the cunning and mendacity which nature and habit had so bountifully bestowed upon them. Seeing this, Livingstone made up his mind to be independent of them as far as possible, and it was with this intention that he subsequently explored the Rovuma River in the hope of finding an alternative route to the Nyassa. Kind as many of the Portuguese had been to him personally, he was determined to oppose the official attitude of the coast authorities, and escape from the trammels which it cast about his efforts.

Before embarking on this new course, he had a duty to fulfil. He took the Makololo back to their homes, and he has told us with what genuine pleasure he preached again to his friends, the people of Sekeletu.

Their journey through the intervening country had been a great success, the people being friendly and hospitable. Mpende, who had in former years been so hostile, received Livingstone now with open arms. But the Makololo were not prospering. Sekeletu had been attacked by leprosy, and kept himself hidden in his hut palace. Pretenders had arisen, and rebellion broken out; the people had not cultivated their fields with their usual diligence, and many were suffering from famine.

Livingstone stayed some time with them, preaching and doctoring and helping them in every way which lay in his power, and in September left them for the east coast. Despite his advice and warnings, despite his efforts and influence, the great warlike Makololo kingdom was breaking up—was already drifting to destruction. A few years afterwards Sekeletu died, and war after war broke over the country, as the various pretenders to supremacy asserted their claims. The usual end of a native empire was at hand. Neighbouring tribes poured in on every side, taking first one part and then another, but always claiming their own independence, and before long there reigned in the rich valley of the Zambesi, from the Victoria Falls to the Barotse country, a score of independent tribes who spoke of Sebituane and Sekeletu and the warlike prowess of the Makololo as persons and matters of history, and who, unlike Livingstone's early friends, were given over to the debasing and fatal practice of the slave trade. The Makololo empire was no more.

A NATIVE DANCE, CENTRAL AFRICA.

CHAPTER VII.

NYASSALAND.

ONE of the results of Livingstone's many letters home, urging the necessity and pointing out the advantages of opening up the Shiré valley and the shores of Lake Nyassa by missionary labour and the founding of a colony, was evidenced early in 1861 by the arrival of several members of the Oxford and Cambridge Mission to Africa. At their head, to guide and control, was Bishop Mackenzie, a hard-working and patient man. With them arrived the *Pioneer*, a steamer sent by the Government in reply to Livingstone's request, and which was to be utilized now for work on the Shiré. The *Ma-Robert* had succumbed to her many ailments by making a final exit on a sandbank near Sena. Livingstone in the meanwhile had written home to his friend Mr. James Young, asking him to purchase another steamer out of the ample funds which "Missionary Travels" had raised for him, and consequently good days appeared to be in store for those who had been exhausting time and strength in their heavily-handicapped struggle for the regeneration of Africa.

As is so often the case, however, the period of his career which Livingstone was on the point of entering was destined to be more laden with trouble and fraught with sorrow than any other time of his life. With the story of a series of disasters and griefs, with the untimely failure of the Universities Mission, and the final recall of the Zambesi Expedition, the ensuing chapter will have to deal.

Up to this point a good deal had been done in spite of all difficulties. The Kongone arm of the Zambesi and an important entrance from the sea had been discovered, navigated, and laid down in charts; the navigability of the Zambesi as far as the Kebrabasa Falls was demonstrated; the great river Shiré had been practically discovered and navigated for the first time. Lake Shirwa was another discovery; and, to cap the whole, there had been found, lying amid the lofty ridges which some four hundred miles inland run parallel with the coast of Eastern Africa, a lake of such extent and character as to alone justify the existence and work of the expedition.

In addition to these discoveries, and the care and skill with which their extent and positions were fixed, many months had been spent in investigating the nature and capabilities of the soil, and the value of the indigenous products. The valley of the Shiré was capable of being made one immense cotton-field, at least four hundred miles in length, and indigo and sugar could be cultivated with perfect success. The Manganja, who inhabited the Shiré valley, raised heavy crops of maize, and led fairly peaceful lives. Provided that it could be demonstrated to them with effect that the white men would buy as much cotton and other crops as they could raise, it was probable that the first principles of civilization and commerce could be permanently introduced; and now, with the advent of the Universities Mission, the exhaustive labour of pioneering would not demand so much of the energies of the expedition as to prevent the constant and continual preaching of the Gospel. With commerce and Christianity advancing side by side, the peaceful conquest of this great land of waterways seemed at hand. The vision indeed was fair, but Livingstone was not destined to behold its fulfilment.

On his arrival at Kongone, Bishop Mackenzie was all anxiety to proceed at once to the Shiré. But as the *Pioneer* was under orders to explore the Rovuma River, with a view to ascertaining whether an alternative water route to the Nyassa existed, and there being no other boat available, his immediate departure was impossible. The Bishop finally agreed to accompany Livingstone in his trip up the Rovuma.

Various delays which had occurred prevented Livingstone from ascending the Rovuma farther than to find the scenery even more beautiful than that of the Zambesi; then the rapid falling of the river warned him that if the *Pioneer* was to get safely back to sea and not meet on some sand or mud-bank the fate of the *Ma-Robert*, it was high time to return. Had he not been accompanied by members of the mission, he would probably have travelled along the banks of the river; but he was induced on their behalf to abandon the attempt, and comfort himself with the resolve to proceed at some future time from the Nyassa eastward until he again struck the river. The *Pioneer* steamed out of the Rovuma, and with Livingstone as pilot and captain rounded Cape Delgado, sailed down the Mozambique coast, and, safely making the Kongone mouth, ascended the Zambesi and Shiré.

While on the Rovuma the *Pioneer* had proved to draw too much water for the tortuous and frequently shallow reaches of African rivers. On the Shiré this defect came out in startling prominence. Many a time she grounded where a vessel drawing but a few inches less would have passed with ease. On one occasion a whole fortnight was employed in getting her off a bank of drifting sand, which she had only just grazed. This single defect caused innumerable delays and a constant toil, in which the unacclimatized missionaries were not far behind. At least, some of them; for it is not to be supposed that among half a dozen men fresh from the luxuries of University and English life, not one would be a laggard, or less enthusiastic for the mission cause while working under an African sun than when contemplating the regeneration of a continent from the persuasive vantage-ground of England. But those who were more fitted for the hard endurance of real mission life behaved nobly. "In hauling the *Pioneer*," wrote Livingstone, "over the shallow places, the Bishop, with Horace Waller and Mr. Scudamore, were ever ready and anxious to lend a hand, and worked as hard as any on board." In all respects save that of draught the *Pioneer* was admirably suited for the work for which she had been built.

In ascending the Shiré, Livingstone realised a truth of which, both then and ever since, the exploration of Africa has yielded abundant proof. Too often, if not invariably, the pluck and suffering of the traveller in opening up new routes and discovering contented if ignorant races have been ill rewarded by the immediate result. For in his steps have come the Arab and half-caste traders, and guided by his discoveries they have laid waste the smiling fields, burnt the villages and towns, and carried off the people in chains to be sold as slaves. Throughout Central Africa this rule has obtained. The advance of the Arabs from the coast has practically depopulated vast tracts of the interior, and even the development of the Congo Free State has not been an unmixed blessing. The Arabs, taking advantage of European philanthropy, have actually been helped in their trade in slaves by the advantages which that great commercial highway has placed in their hands. Now, as in the days of Livingstone, the great question remains unsolved: How can we benefit Africa and not benefit the Arab?

With deep disappointment Livingstone piloted the combined forces of the expedition and mission up the Shiré. When near the Murchison Cataracts they met, Livingstone says, "a long line of manacled men, women, and children. The black owners, armed with muskets and bedecked with various articles of finery, marched jauntily in the front, middle, and rear of the line; some of them blowing exultant notes out of long tin horns. They seemed to feel that they were doing a very noble thing, and might proudly march with an air of triumph. But the instant the fellows caught a glimpse of the English they darted off like mad into the forest." This was certainly a compliment to the nation which Livingstone represented, and one which would never have been paid to the Portuguese. The slaves were released from their chains, and taken charge of by the mission.

Shortly after this, for the first time during the Doctor's many years of travel in Africa, he was fired upon by the natives. The party had been freeing a number of slaves whom they had met, and, ascertaining that the Ajawa, a tribe near the Zomba range, had been actively engaged in raiding among the peaceful Manganja for slaves, it was resolved to pay the chief of the Ajawa a visit, with a view to weaning him from his nefarious ways. The path led through a country in the active stage of devastation. The smoke from burning villages arose to heaven, the shrieks of widowed and wounded women fell on their ears. The Ajawa received the party with a heavy fire, and in self-defence it had to be returned. "Had we known better," says Livingstone, "the effect of slavery and murder on the temper of these bloodthirsty marauders, we should have tried messages and presents before going near them."

A few days afterwards the mission fixed their first station at Magomero, the town of the chief Chigunda, and which lay on the eastern slope of the Zomba range; and the members of the expedition bade them farewell. By way of parting advice, and in answer to an inquiry of the Bishop's as to his protecting *vi et armis* the Manganjas from the marauding Ajawa, Livingstone declared most emphatically that such a policy would lead to mischief. "You will be oppressed by their importunities, but do not interfere with native quarrels." Had such advice been heeded, the troubles which subsequently beset the mission would probably have been avoided.

The remaining history of the Universities Mission in the basin of the Shiré may be briefly related here. On Livingstone's departure, the Bishop and his coadjutors commenced the requisite preliminary operations. The Bishop set to work to learn the language, Mr. Waller undertook the building of the necessary houses, and Mr. Scudamore started an infant school. After a time they became seriously involved with the natives, and in the course of some aggressive dealings with the slave-trading Ajawa and others suffered much from exposure. The anxiety and toil, coupled with the fact that the unhealthy season was bringing with it the usual series of ills, led to the unfortunate death of the Bishop, from fever, while endeavouring to descend the Shiré. His companion, Mr. Burrup, who was also suffering severely from dysentery, had just strength enough to stagger to the grave which their Makololo servants had made, and there repeat some portions of the Service for the Burial of the Dead. Mr. Burrup was then carried back to Magomero by the Makololo, and soon after died. The behaviour of these servants was splendid. For three long weeks they sat beside the Bishop's mat, as without medicine or proper food he slowly grew weaker and succumbed. Their devotion to Mr. Burrup was as great; and, indeed, throughout their connection with the mission these men, who had learnt the character of the white man from so great a teacher and example as Dr. Livingstone, served their masters with conspicuous loyalty and zeal.

In April 1862, Mr. Waller arrived at Shupanga, at the head of the Zambesi delta, to collect provisions. The depredations of the Ajawa and a drought, which occurs every few years in this region, had made food so scarce that many of the people were starving, and the missionaries were suffering from diseases resulting from poor and insufficient food. Having hired and loaded a number of canoes, Waller reascended the Shiré, only to discover that the remnant of the mission at Magomero had fled down to the low valley of the Shiré, and taken up their quarters with Chibisa, a friendly chief. This was a most unhealthy site, but in spite of Waller's remonstrances all preferred to stay by the Shiré rather than return to the uplands of Zomba. Within a short space of time three of the party died; and Tozer, who arrived soon after to succeed Mackenzie as bishop, determined to abandon the mission on the Shiré, and make Zanzibar its headquarters. And this, to Livingstone's unspeakable grief, he did. The Doctor, writing to his friend Maclear, at the Cape, said he felt inclined to "sit down and cry." The hopes and labours of years seemed shattered in a moment. "I see that if you go," he wrote to the Bishop, "the last ray of hope for this wretched trodden-down people disappears, and I again from the bottom of my heart entreat you to reconsider the matter."

The matter was not reconsidered, however; and Mackenzie's successor, while enjoying the style and title of "Bishop of Central Africa," contented himself with applying his own interpretation to the words, confining his residence and labours to the island of Zanzibar, and getting a distant view of the continent on a fine day.

In the meanwhile, on leaving the mission at Magomero, the Doctor with Charles Livingstone and John Kirk had started for Nyassa. The *Pioneer* was left at Chibisa's, at the foot of the Murchison Cataracts, and a small boat was carried along the banks for some forty miles until they could put it on the upper Shiré. Thence they proceeded to the Nyassa, arriving at the lake on the 2nd of September.

The first point of interest noticed was a long promontory, projecting, like a tongue, in a northerly direction from the extreme south of the lake, and which they named Cape Maclear, in honour of the Doctor's old friend, the Astronomer Royal at Capetown. This promontory is mountainous, and no bottom could be got, at that time, with a line of thirty-five fathoms. The Nyassa, in fact, was to prove a very different lake from the Ngami.

The mountains on the west of the lake are the lofty edges of the central plateau; those on the east, afterwards called the Livingstone Range, are isolated. The months of September and October which Livingstone spent on the lake were stormy, and these mountain ranges drew down upon its surface fierce and sudden gusts of wind. The squalls would come with a sudden rush, only discernible by the white line of leaping breakers before they swooped down upon the small boat with a roar, and often was Livingstone caught and detained on his *détour* of the lake by these dangerous storms.

"Never before in Africa," he writes, "have we seen anything like the dense population on the shores of Lake Nyassa. In the southern part there was an almost unbroken chain of villages. On the beach of well-nigh every little sandy bay dark crowds were standing, gazing at the novel sight of a boat under sail; and wherever we landed we were surrounded in a few seconds by hundreds of men, women, and children, who hastened to have a stare at the 'chirombo'—wild animals. To see the animals feed was the greatest attraction: never did the Zoological Society's lions or monkeys draw more sightseers than we did. The wondering multitude crowded round us at meal-times and formed a thicket of dark bodies, all looking on, apparently, with the deepest interest; but they good-naturedly kept each other to a line we made on the sand, and left us room to dine. Twice they went the length of lifting up the edge of our sail, which we used as a tent, as boys do the curtains of travelling menageries at home. . . . At one village only were they impudent, but *they* were 'elevated' by beer. . . . They cultivate the soil pretty extensively, and grow large quantities of rice and sweet potatoes, as well as maize, mapira, and millet. In the north, however, cassava is the staple product, which, with fish kept till the flavour is high, constitutes the main support of the inhabitants."

Livingstone found the natives addicted to the use of the pelele, the horizontal ring ornament for the upper lip, and tattooed from head to foot. Some of the tribes raised up knobs on the skin of the face, which gave the appearance of leprosy to many of the older people. It was the fashion among them and most of the tribes of the Zambesi to cut their really fine teeth to points like the teeth of cats. Everywhere the visitors were received with kindness, save and except when they cut across the path of the slave trader. The people then became impudent and dishonest; their first question was, "Have you come to buy slaves?" and on being told that the English never bought slaves the inquirers became contemptuous, and even refused to sell food. It was near one of the "crossing-places" on the Nyassa that Livingstone was robbed, for the first time in Africa—a number of personal articles of clothing and toilet being stolen at night.

While Livingstone struck inland for a short trip, the boat with his brother and Dr. Kirk proceeded northward some distance; and where the mountainous coasts seemed, owing to a haze, to draw together, they placed the northern extremity of the lake—that is, about 11° south. As a matter of fact a more careful survey, un-

SHUPANGA HOUSE, IN WHICH MRS. LIVINGSTONE DIED.

dertaken later on by Mr. E. D. Young, established the limit as being about $9\frac{1}{2}°$ south—a clear gain in length to this inland sea of a degree and a half, or rather over a hundred miles.

Finding no outlet from the Nyassa to the Rovuma, and having exhausted their goods, at the end of October Livingstone left the lake, and, descending the Shiré, rejoined the *Pioneer* below the Cataracts. Several delays occurred, and the steamer lay at one shoal for five long weeks.

On arriving at the Portuguese settlements on the Zambesi, he expected to be questioned about the freeing of the slaves whom he and the Bishop had met up the Shiré. But only one remark was made; he was asked, "You took the governor's slaves, didn't you?" Livingstone replied that he certainly freed some gangs he had encountered; and goes on, in his book, to say that "the Portuguese of Tete, from the governor downwards, were extensively engaged in slaving."

The 30th of January, 1862, was a great day for the Doctor. H.M.S. *Gorgon* appeared off the mouth of the Kongone, and Livingstone, steaming out in the *Pioneer*, went on board, to find his wife, and a steamer which he had ordered through James Young, and which was intended for work on the Nyassa. Mrs. Livingstone had been in England since parting with her husband at Capetown, but had now come out to join him in his work. She was not to help him for long.

The unhealthy season was at its height, and the party were delayed at Shupanga by the slow process of conveying the many sections of the *Lady Nyassa* to that place and there fitting them together. The surrounding low land, rank with vegetation, and reeking from the late rainy season, exhaled the malarious poison in enormous quantities. On the 21st of April, Mrs. Livingstone fell ill—on the 27th she died.

Although Livingstone touches on this great grief but slightly in his journal—and which is consistent with his almost complete suppression of personal and religious feelings in that book—the death of his wife was a great blow. In his private journal we find evidence of his sorrowing, though not as one without hope. Here are some extracts:—

"I loved her when I married her, and the longer I lived with her I loved her the more. . . . It is the first heavy stroke I have suffered, and quite takes away my strength. . . . My Mary, how often we have longed for a quiet home, since you and I were cast adrift at Kolobeng! . . . God pity the poor children, who were all tenderly attached to her; and I am left alone in the world by one whom I felt to be a part of myself. . . . She rests by the large baobab tree at Shupanga. . . . Vividly do I remember my first passage down in 1856, passing Shupanga with the impression that it was a beautiful spot. . . . In some other spot I may have looked at, my own resting-place may be allotted. I have often wished that it might be in some far-off still deep forest, where I may sleep sweetly till the resurrection morn."

The blow was crushing, and for a while Livingstone was quite bewildered. Gradually his old energy returned, and with something of his old vigour he superintended the launching of the *Lady Nyassa*. But again delay had worked against success, for the rainy season was past, and there was no prospect of the steamer being able to ascend the Shiré till the end of the year. Once more, therefore, did Livingstone sail up the Mozambique coast and enter the Rovuma. After exploring about a hundred and fifty miles of that river, and ascertaining in spite of the hostility of the natives that it had no direct connection with the Nyassa, he returned to the Zambesi, and in January, 1863, once again entered the Shiré.

The desolation worked by the slave trade during his absence was appalling. The river banks which had formerly been so populous were now silent; all the villages had been burnt, and their inhabitants killed or carried away into captivity. Here and there they came upon some wretched survivor, supporting himself on fish or wild berries, but the population was either dead or gone. "The sight and smell of dead bodies was everywhere. Many skeletons lay beside the path, where in their weakness they had fallen and expired. ... The corpse of a boy floated past the ship; a monstrous crocodile rushed at it with the speed of a greyhound, caught it, and shook it as a terrier dog does a rat. Others dashed at the prey, each with his powerful tail causing the water to churn and froth, as he furiously tore off a piece. In a few seconds it was all gone. The sight was frightful to behold."

As usual, in the path of the slave trader had followed a famine. The labour of the country being removed without warning, the crops are not gathered in, and the seed is not sown; and those who have escaped the cruel mercies of the trader die of the lingering pains of starvation. After describing the hideous sights which the Shiré valley presented at that time, Livingstone writes: "The sight of this desert, but eighteen months ago a well-peopled valley, now literally strewn with human bones, forced the conviction upon us that unless the slave trade—that monster iniquity which has so long brooded over Africa—is put down, lawful commerce cannot be established."

While the *Lady Nyassa* was being taken to pieces, and a road alongside the Cataracts under construction, the Zambesi Expedition was recalled. This was another blow to Livingstone's plans, though hardly to his hopes; he had long expected it. The grounds upon which the recall was issued were that the expedition had proved more costly than had been estimated, and the return was not adequate to the expense. At the bottom of this, the strained relations between the English and Portuguese Governments had a good deal of influence in the matter; and, although public feeling at home was aroused on the slave-trading question, there was some complication, according to the diplomatists, in the manner in which the expedition was dealing or said to be dealing with its practical solution.

Of the value of the work of the expedition there

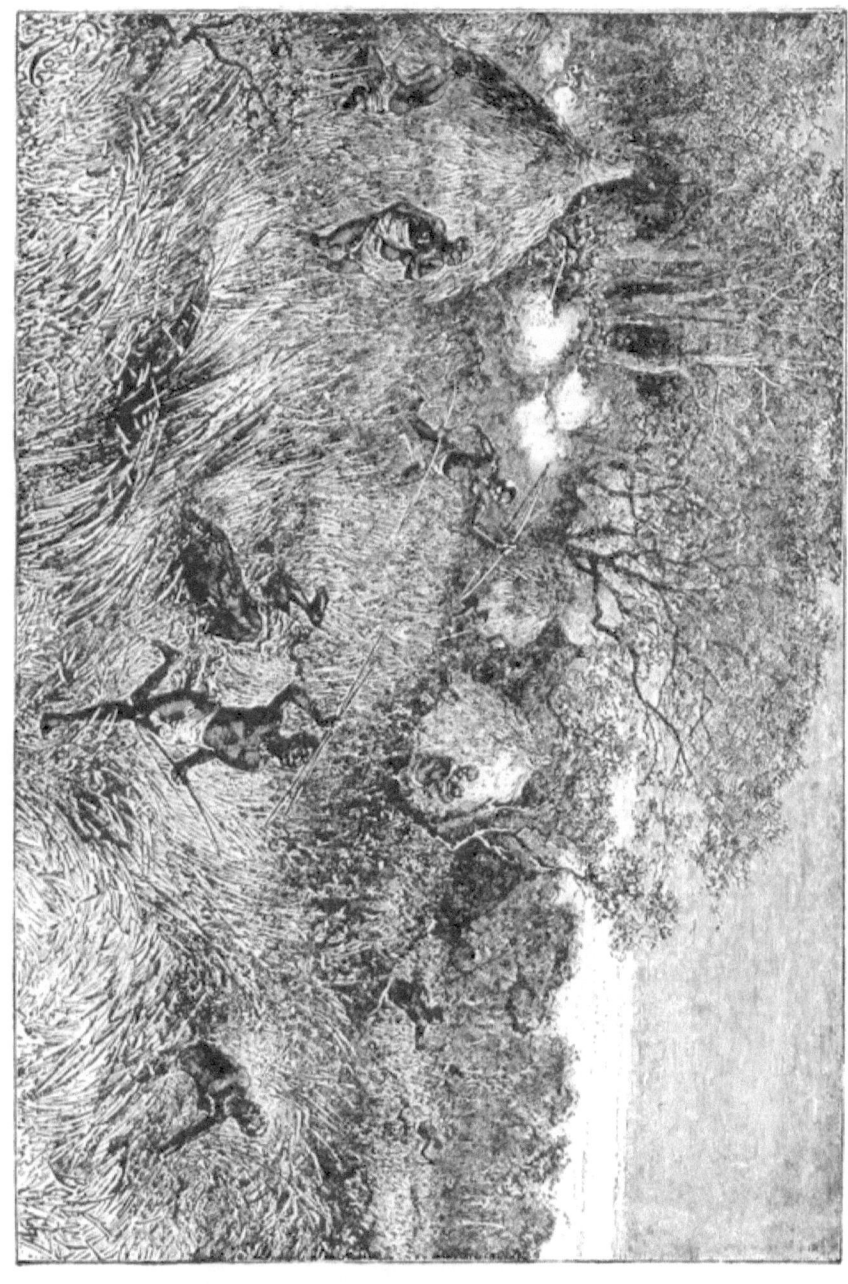

ARAB SLAVERS' ATTACK ON A VILLAGE.

could be no question, and a brief summary of its main achievements was given at the beginning of this chapter. Since then the great Nyassa Lake had been navigated, and the possibility of a water-route to it by the Rovuma negatived. The salubrity of the elevated country around the lake and the higher points along the Shiré valley, and not directly on the river, had been established, and the extreme fertility of the soil proved beyond doubt. And last, and also first, the labours of the expedition had tracked the slaver to his inland haunts, laid bare the cruelties and evils which followed in his train, and pointed out the way to diminish his influence and circumvent his cunning. In doing all this, Livingstone and his companions had proved to the natives that there were white men who neither bought nor sold their fellow-creatures, and to whom the villainies of the slave trade were detestable. He had gained for the name of the English both the respect and affection of the natives.

He had done this, but he was not content. Duty, as he saw it, beckoned him into the interior, led him on to further labour. There was to be no turning back for him. In a letter to Mr. Waller he said: "I don't know whether I am to go on the shelf or not. If I do, I make Africa the shelf." The expedition might be recalled and its work be finished, but Livingstone had not yet fulfilled his self-imposed task, and his work was to go on. The hand of duty was beckoning to him from the heart of Africa, and he now prepared to obey it.

A VIEW ON LAKE TANGANIKA.

CHAPTER VIII.

INDIA AND ENGLAND.

BEFORE he could penetrate Africa again with any chance of success, Livingstone well knew that he must raise funds. There were two ways of doing this: first, by selling the *Lady Nyassa*, which had cost him nearly £6,000; and, in the event of not doing that, by going to England and raising money there. He resolved to try the first.

The Portuguese authorities, on hearing that the steamer was for sale, offered to buy it, but Livingstone refused to sell it to them, knowing that it would soon be subserving their purposes by helping in the slave traffic. He then sailed up the coast to Zanzibar, and here again he had some offers, but the sums were considered absurdly small, and he determined to try and sell her in a better market. With this object in view, he made up his mind to sail the little ship across the Indian Ocean to Bombay.

On the last day of April 1864, he started on this perilous voyage. Though warned that the breaking of the monsoon would probably take place before he made port, Livingstone would not be deterred. It is likely enough that, having seen the steamer ride out a heavy cyclone off the Mozambique coast without receiving any injury, he had formed a high opinion of her seaworthiness; and it is certain that she had never shown any cause why that character was not really deserved.

The distance was some two thousand five hundred miles; and though Livingstone had calculated that he might make the passage in something under twenty days it really occupied forty-five days! Himself skipper, he had three Europeans as sailor, stoker, and carpenter; seven Zambesians, ignorant of seamanship, though accustomed to river navigation; and two lads. Of Chuma, one of these lads, we shall hear again. The Doctor had fourteen tons of coal put in the hold for use in calms and when on a dangerous lee coast.

These natives turned out admirable sailors; for in the first week or so, when two of the Englishmen were laid up with fever, they learnt and performed all the simple duties of seamen. Their "skipper" writes of them: "So eager were they to do their duty, that only one of them lay down from sea-sickness during the whole voyage. They took in and set sail very cleverly in a short time, and would climb out along a boom, reeve a rope through the block, and come back with the rope in their teeth, though at each lurch the performer was dipped in the sea."

The Doctor made his course first northerly and along the east coast, in order to take advantage of a strong current, and then in a north-easterly direction to Bombay. But where he expected to find a steady breeze he found calms; and, what with constant calms and currents almost the whole way across, progress was but slow, and patience extremely difficult. Indeed, at times, he became very downcast, and wrote in his journal: "I often feel as if I am to die on this voyage, and wish I had sent the accounts to the Government, as also my chart of the Zambesi." Elsewhere he wrote: "Our epitaph would be 'Left Zanzibar on 30th of April, 1864, and never more heard of.'"

About a month after setting out the little ship encountered a heavy gale, which tore the sails from their bolt-ropes and sent her plunging "nose under" through the big waves, or rolling broadside over into their trough. Heavy squalls of rain became more frequent as the days went by, and in one of these the foresail was torn to ribbons—no slight loss. Day after day dawned wet and scowling, and the Doctor, knowing that the breaking of the monsoon was due, became anxious.

The monsoon dreaded was, of course, that from the south-west. The constant south-westerly wind which blows across the Indian Ocean during the summer months of the year gathers up an enormous amount of moisture as it sweeps over that greatly evaporating ocean, and on coming in contact with the cooler air above the highlands which line the western coast of India, this quantity of moisture assumes the form of dense black clouds, which rush over the Western Ghâts and Nilgiris, rolling thunder and forking lightning over the lofty peaks and down the mountain gorges, and finally bursting in a deluge of rain. Day after day it rains incessantly. Then there is a pause, only to be followed in July by more rain. The rainy season is now at its height. Gradually the rain ceases until, in September, the south-west monsoon departs, as it came, in a wild fury of thunder and lightning, and is succeeded by the north-east monsoon and its dry cool season.

Well might Livingstone dread the breaking of this weather-demon over the little *Lady Nyassa*, and thankful indeed was he when, on June 11th, he sighted land. Both wind and sea were high at the time, and the horizon hazy, but he held on his course, steering by compass and chart. "Wind whistled through the rigging loudly, and we made but little progress steaming.

About midnight a white patch reported. Seemed a shoal, but none is marked on chart. At daylight we found ourselves abreast high land at least five hundred feet above sea-level. Hills not so beautifully coloured as those in Africa. We had calms after the squalls, and this morning the sea is as smooth as glass, and a thick haze over the land. A scum as of dust on the face of the water. . . . We came to lightship. It was so hazy inland we could see nothing whatever; then took the direction by chart, and steered right into Bombay most thankfully. I mention God's good providence over me, and beg that He may accept my spared life for His service."

Truly a remarkable voyage! This landsman, this missionary to the people of Central Africa, navigating a little ship, against calm and current, through gale and squall, full two thousand five hundred miles, and steering right into port, safe and sound, and, undoubtedly, most thankfully. He was indeed the type of all that is practical and able, a master-spirit, and yet a child in the hands of his God. Fearless, eager, never too old to learn, though always willing and capable of teaching. If ever there was an "all-round man," that man was David Livingstone.

After a brief sojourn at Bombay, where he received much kindness from Sir Bartle Frere, the then governor, Dr. Wilson, the eminent missionary, and many others, Livingstone left the steamer "for sale" in dock, and sailed on the mail-packet for England, arriving there on the 23rd of July.

Nothing but kindness awaited him. His old friend, Sir Roderick Murchison, welcomed him as a brother. Lord Palmerston, the Earl of Shaftesbury, the Duke of Argyll, and many men of the highest importance as well as rank, paid him every attention. He was much comforted by conversations he had with Palmerston, whose views on the slave trade coincided with his. He soon paid his old friend, James Young, a visit, and thence he went to Hamilton to see his mother and his children. Thence to Inveraray, to stay with the Duke of Argyll; and from there round by Ulva, the home of his Highland ancestors, to Glasgow, where he made the acquaintance of the veteran Dr. Duff, then lately returned from India, and so back again to Hamilton.

In August an old friend of Kolobeng days, Mr. Webb, of Newstead Abbey, invited him to make his home there, and though the invitation was accepted for only a short period, Livingstone stayed with Mr. Webb and his wife nearly the whole of the time he was in England, and wrote his book, " The Zambesi and its Tributaries," in the comfort and with the conveniences which they placed at his disposal.

This book was not entirely Livingstone's work, for he incorporated the journal of his brother Charles, and, indeed, had not Dr. Kirk intended to publish a separate book on the natural history of the Zambesi and Shiré, his notes also would have been included and his name appeared on the title-page. Livingstone never grudged any man his meed, and these two able assistants always received the fullest recognition at his hands. Chiefly through Livingtone's exertions his brother received the appointment of consul at Fernando Po, and Kirk was made consul-general at Zanzibar. Their own claims, however, for distinct recognition were great; and when Dr. Kirk afterwards received the Gold Medal of the Royal Geographical Society, "for his long-continued and unremitting services to geography," together with the Grand Cross of the Order of SS. Michael and George, as a proof of his sovereign's approbation, he received no more than was his due.

Early in 1865 Sir Roderick Murchison entered into correspondence with Livingstone with regard to future labours in Africa. However much Murchison might be in accord with the Doctor on matters geographical, on questions missionary he held totally different views. This comes out in a letter he wrote about this time, from which the following is an extract:—

"Quite irrespective of missionaries or political affairs, there is at this moment a question of intense geographical interest to be settled—namely, the watershed or watersheds of South Africa. Now, if you would really like to be the person to finish off your remarkable career by completing such a survey, unshackled by other avocations than those of the geographical explorer, I should be delighted to consult my friends of the Society, and take the best steps to promote such an enterprise."

Consequent upon this Livingstone entered a note in his journal, which admirably establishes his views of the question. "Answered Sir Roderick about going out. Said I could only feel in the way of duty by working as a missionary." In his letter he had said, " My inclination leads me to prefer to have intercourse with the people, and do what I can by talking to enlighten them on the slave trade, and give them some idea of our religion." This is but harking back to his original idea, when working among the Bakwains, of a band of missionaries, in twos or threes or even singly, passing through and through, up and down, in and out the whole country, sowing the seed far and wide, and publishing the glad tidings indeed abroad. And yet there were not wanting those who said he had merged the missionary in the explorer!

Writing later to James Young, and referring to this correspondence, he reiterated his statement : " I would not consent to go simply as a geographer, but as a missionary, and do geography by the way, because I feel I am in the way of duty when trying either to enlighten these poor people or open their land to lawful commerce."

"Duty"—that was the word, the motive. It was the

motto of his life. It led him to break up his peaceful home at Kolobeng, induced him to leave the Makololo, among whom he had found friendship and plenty, and risk the perils of the journey to Loanda; it had brought him back again to Linyanti, and thence away down the Zambesi to Quilimane; it had urged him to the work of the expedition, and to assume the most irksome post —that of navigating the boat, while the others held converse with the natives, or examined the resources of the country; it had taken him away from the seclusion of his sorrow, when his "beloved Mary Moffat" was laid to rest at Shupanga; it had roused him from his own bed of sickness to cheer and lead; brought him in trustfulness across the stormy ocean; and, now, compelled him to oppose his best friend in a matter on which, in all other points, they were agreed.

While this correspondence was passing, Livingstone went to Hamilton for the purpose of attending a prize-giving at his son's school. Called upon, as usual, to make a speech, he spoke to the children in his simple kindly fashion, pointing out how necessary it was to be practical in all things, and concluding with an earnest injunction to "fear God and work hard." This incident is mentioned here as having given an impetus and direction to the life of a lad who heard him on that occasion, and to whom further reference will be made in this book. The work of Frederick Stanley Arnot is one of the most characteristic portions of the legacy which Livingstone has left to us.

In the spring of 1865 he was offered, without so much as even a hint from him that he would care for it, the appointment of British consul in Central Africa. With a parsimony and narrowness of view which has characterized the relations of various Governments with some of the very best men of this generation, this offer, spontaneously made, was coupled with the stipulation that no pay was to be attached to the post, and that no pension need be expected. When some influential friends of the Doctor remonstrated with the Foreign Office authorities, it was intimated that a salary would be granted when Livingstone settled permanently somewhere—an intimation which disclosed a painful ignorance of the duties and difficulties accompanying such a post in so enormous a region. But Livingstone, though hurt by the lack of generosity, was too enthusiastic for Africa to hesitate. In Africa he knew the natives had never heard of Cabinets, General Elections, or Chancellors of the Exchequer. All that had been done for them appeared in the light of personal achievements and individual influence. Whether he was paid or not for his labours, the poor African whom he yearned to benefit would accept or reject his efforts and his teaching on purely personal grounds. So he determined to accept the appointment.

Now came the Geographical Society's commission. Their object was to ascertain the watershed of South Central Africa, and of course to determine whether the ultimate sources of the Nile were to be found among the hills or lakes of the interior south of the point where Speke and Grant had seen that river coming from the Victoria Nyanza. They wished also to settle the connection or proximity of the Nyassa with the Tanganika. All this they wanted done by Livingstone, and thus it is that we find him starting for Africa with a twofold purpose.

If we quote his own words, a clear idea will be gained as to his own intentions: "I purpose to go inland, north of the territory which the Portuguese in Europe claim, and endeavour to commence that system on the east which has been so eminently successful on the west coast—a system combining the repressive efforts of Her Majesty's cruisers with lawful trade and Christian missions, the moral and material results of which have been so gratifying."

INDIA AND ENGLAND.

This referred to the duties of his consulship, and he then proceeds to describe the work he had undertaken to do for the Geographical Society: "I hope to ascend the Rovuma or some other river north of Cape Delgado, and, in addition to my other work, shall strive, by passing along the northern end of Lake Nyassa and round the southern end of Lake Tanganika, to ascertain the watershed of that part of Africa. In so doing, I have no wish to unsettle what with so much toil and danger was accomplished by Speke and Grant, but rather to confirm their illustrious discoveries."

One of the last entries in Livingstone's journal as he was bidding farewell to his friends and on the point of leaving London for ever may be appropriately quoted here: "We have been with Dr. and Mrs. Hamilton for some time—good, gracious people. The Lord bless them and their household! Dr. Kirk and Mr. Waller go down to Folkestone to-morrow, and take leave of us there. This is very kind. The Lord puts it into their hearts to show kindness, and blessed be His Name!"

THE MISSION STATION, LIVINGSTONIA, NYASSA LAKE.

CHAPTER IX.

NILE OR CONGO?

THE unsold *Lady Nyassa* led Livingstone back to Bombay, and his presence there enabled him to find a purchaser for the vessel which he had bought out of the profits of his book, and on which he had centred so many hopes for the tribes around Lake Nyassa—hopes not to be realised in his own lifetime, though largely fulfilled at this day. The vessel had cost him nearly £6,000, but the highest price he could obtain for it was £2,300; and as Livingstone temporarily lodged that sum in an Indian bank, which subsequently failed, the whole of the original cost was lost.

From Bombay he sailed to Zanzibar, bearing to the Sultan a letter of introduction, couched in the most cordial language, from Sir Bartle Frere, the governor; and also, as a present from that official to the Zanzibar potentate, the steamship in which the Doctor made the passage. After some delay at Zanzibar, he was conveyed by a British gunboat to Mikindany Bay, some twenty odd miles north of the mouth of the river Rovuma. On the 24th of March, 1866, he set foot again on African soil—a soil he was destined to tramp southward and northward, eastward and westward, without intermission, and though often weary yet never wavering, until a Higher Purpose led him to Ilala, and thence revealed to him another country—even a heavenly.

When he started from the east coast he had thirty-six followers, of whom thirteen were Indian Sepoys, ten hailed from Johanna, one of the Comoro Islands, nine were Nassick boys trained in India, two belonged to Shupanga, and two were Waiyaus. One of the Shupanga men was Susi, and of the Waiyaus one was Chuma. These men will be heard of again.

The Doctor also took with him three tame Indian buffaloes, six camels, and several mules and donkeys, in order to test the range and result of the bite of the tse-tse. Unfortunately these poor animals were so roughly treated by some of his men that the experiment proved of no value. Its attempt, however, is but another link in the long chain of evidence which has placed before our eyes a unique example of unwavering purpose in Livingstone's endeavours to benefit the African.

As he slowly ascended the Rovuma, delayed continually by these animals in his train, the miserable character of the majority of his followers became unpleasantly evident. He suffered so much, indeed, from the rascally behaviour of the Sepoys that he finally sent them back to the coast. Some of the Johanna men stole from the natives of the villages; others injured the crops by carelessly allowing the camels and buffaloes to stray into them; others, again, would hire natives to carry their burdens for them, assuring them that the Doctor would pay. Sometimes when on the march they would lag behind and lie down to sleep by the roadside; at others, they would actually throw away portions of their loads to make them lighter; one man had twenty pounds of tea to carry, and he deliberately reduced that moderate burden to five pounds by throwing away the rest. Another calmly appropriated a number of yards of cloth from his load, and packed them in his own bundle. Having lagged behind upon one occasion, they killed a young buffalo—the last of the buffaloes—and ate it. Upon coming up with Livingstone the explanation volunteered by the Sepoys was that a "tiger" had devoured it. Yes—there was no doubt about it—they saw the tiger. Livingstone queried, "Did you see the stripes of the tiger?" Yes—they all had, most distinctly. There being no striped tiger in Africa, the bottom of this excuse was very soon knocked out.

As he advanced along the banks of the Rovuma, or deflected his course into the neighbouring country, Livingstone found the soil invariably fertile and the land well watered. But the slave trade had already depopulated many districts, and on several occasions there was the greatest difficulty in getting food. Proofs, if proofs were needed, of this cursed traffic became more and more common. On one day they would find the corpse of a woman who had been tightly tied to a tree and left to starve, since she was too weak to keep up with the caravan. The next day, a half-starved corpse would be found lying in their path—the body of a poor wretch who had been done to death with an axe. Here two men lay, still fettered in the *goree*, or taming-stick, which plays so great a part in the slave trade. And there the corpse of a mere babe, who had been flung into the long grass by the wayside in order that its mother's strength should not be overtaxed.

On arriving in July at Mtarika's, Livingstone reproached the chief for allowing his beautiful country to be robbed of its people, and the long stretches of once cultivated fields to lapse again into jungle. Mtarika, though of unprepossessing appearance, took the reproof in good part, merely stipulating that the Doctor gave the same salutary advice to the other chiefs. Though perfectly willing to sell their countrymen into slavery, they did not like to be associated with the terrible mortality which attended the process; and, like a great many other people in continents other than Africa, their logic was of that convenient nature which justifies the action, while it ignores the immediate result.

Leaving Mtarika's, whose large settlement was situated in hilly and fertile country, and at a point in the Rovuma where that river was about a hundred yards in width, the Doctor worked his way south through a depopulated district, where food was consequently difficult to obtain, and arrived at Mataka's ten days later. This chief he found to be of an amiable character, and during the fortnight he stayed at his settlement Livingstone received unstinted hospitality, and, on his part, repaid it by much good advice as to the better cultivation of the country, and the practical wisdom of forswearing the slave trade. "One day," he writes in his journal, "calling at Mataka's, I found, as usual, a large crowd of idlers, who always respond with a laugh to everything he utters as wit. He asked, if he went to Bombay, what ought he to take to secure some gold? I replied, 'Ivory;' he rejoined, 'Would slaves not be a good speculation?' I replied that if he took slaves there for sale they would put him in prison. The idea of the great Mataka in 'chokee' made him wince, and the laugh turned for once against him."

On the 8th of August the Doctor once more reached

Lake Nyassa—this time at that point on the eastern shore where the river Misinje empties its waters into the lake. Here he rested, wrote up his journal, and worked out a number of astronomical observations which he had made. Among the notes he entered at this date are the following:—

"Some men have come down from Mataka's, and report the arrival of an Englishmen with cattle for me. 'He has two eyes behind as well as two in front.' This is enough of news for a while!"

"Mokalaosé has his little afflictions, and he tells me of them. A wife ran away. I asked how many he had; he told me twenty in all: I then thought he had nineteen too many. He answered with the usual reason, 'But who would cook for strangers if I had but one?'"

"A leopard took a dog out of a house next to ours; he had bitten a man before, but not mortally."

"The fear which the English have inspired in the Arab slave traders is rather inconvenient. All flee before me as if I had the plague, and I cannot in consequence transmit letters to the coast or get across the lake."

"I made very good blue ink from the juice of a berry, the fruit of a creeper."

"The poodle-dog Chitané is rapidly changing the colour of its hair. All the parts corresponding to the ribs and neck are rapidly becoming red; the majority of country dogs are of this colour."

Livingstone had left the country of the Waiyau, and was now among tribes of the Manganja race. Of the latter he says: "They have great manes of hair, and but little if any of the prognathous in the profile. Their bodies and limbs are very well made, and the countenance of the men is often very pleasant. The women are very plain and lumpy, but exceedingly industrious in their gardens from early morning till about 11 A.M., then from 3 P.M. till dark, or pounding corn and grinding it; the men make twine or nets by day, and are at their fisheries in the evenings and nights. They build the huts, the women plaster them."

"A lion visited a woman early yesterday morning, and ate most of her undisturbed."

After crossing a number of small rivers, Livingstone arrived at the southern extremity of the lake on the 13th of September, and in his journal on that day we find this entry: "Many hopes have been disappointed here. Far down on the right bank of the Zambesi lies the dust of her whose death changed all my future prospects; and now, instead of a check being given to the slave trade by lawful commerce on the lake, slave dhows prosper."

Shortly after this, the Doctor met with one of those morasses he subsequently encountered so often, and which he well named "sponges." An African sponge is a bog, formed by many deposits of foliage, twigs, branches, and the like on river sand. In course of time these deposits rot and form a rich black humus, which in dry weather cracks in all directions in narrow but deep fissures. In the wet season, however, this loamy humus becomes soft slush, and moves like a body of water over the sand. The obstacle which such a mass, spread over perhaps the only level tract of country within many miles' reach, would present to a traveller can be very readily imagined.

In the latter end of September, the Johanna men, with Musa at their head, deserted the Doctor in a body. They had behaved in an atrocious manner, and given him infinite trouble from the very first; and now, owing to a report that the tribes ahead of their intended route were extremely hostile, they laid down their loads and calmly walked off. "No good country that," Musa declared. "I want to go back to Johanna to see my father and mother and son."

Livingstone's comment is characteristic: "They have been such inveterate thieves that I am not sorry to get rid of them." But he did not know at the time what Musa's cunning and careful consideration for "number one" were capable of. For, being desirous of getting his pay on arriving at Zanzibar, he concocted a "cock and bull" story in which he depicted the fearful hostility of the natives as culminating in a ferocious attack upon the whole party, and the murder of the Doctor. Into this narrative was woven a deal of circumstantial detail, and when the news reached England the greatest consternation and grief were felt. There were not wanting those who disbelieved the report, however; and among them were Horace Waller, who had known Livingstone and worked with him on the Zambesi and Shiré as well as in England, and Edward D. Young, who had also done good service on the Zambesi. The latter gentleman was commissioned by the Geographical Society to search for Livingstone, and he performed his work in so admirable a manner as to prove beyond all doubt that Musa was, as he had supposed him to be, a liar. For, according to this fellow, Livingstone had gone round the north of the lake, and not the south; whereas Mr. Young not only found men at the south end of the lake who remembered the Doctor well, but also learnt from Marenga, the chief, all about Livingstone's sojourn there, and the whole story of the heartless desertion and cowardice of the Johanna men.

And all the while Livingstone, with a diminished following, was slowly journeying northward to the Tanganika. Here is a note which occurs in his journal at this period: "As for our general discourse, we mention our relationship to our Father; His love to all His children—the guilt of selling any of His children—the consequence. We mention the Bible—future state—prayer; advise union, that they should unite as one family to expel enemies, who came first as slave traders, and ended by leaving the country a wilderness."

The question of the watershed of this part of Africa was decided by Livingstone. He first discovered that the Tanganika did not belong to the same drainage system as the Nyassa, and then that a whole chain of lakes, extending from Bemba or Bangweolo northward, was traversed by one great river, which rose, as the Chambeze, in the uplands between Nyassa and the Tanganika, which issued successively from Bangweolo as the Luapala, from Lake Moero as the Luvwa, and from Lake Kamolondo as the Lualaba. Within a comparatively short distance of this point it flows past Nyangwé, an Arab settlement in the now depopulated Manyuema, and this spot is the northern limit of Livingstone's investigations into the river, which largely occupied the labour of the last years of his life, and which he believed would ultimately be found to flow into the Nile. And yet he would often pause and wonder if, after all, the Lualaba turned sharply to the west, and flowed with great rapidity, and possibly—owing to the elevated edge of the central plateau—over lofty falls, to the west coast, finally entering the Atlantic Ocean as the Congo. Might it not even, since the natives declared it flowed north for ever and ever, reach into the far Soudan, and form a mighty contributary stream of the Niger? But he would turn away time and again from these conjectures, and believe, as he hoped, that it must ultimately prove to be the Nile. That river, famed in sacred as well as profane history, had an alluring charm for him; and the thought that it might be his part to uncover the hidden sources of the river which had witnessed the wonderful works of the Pharaohs, and the still more marvellous acts in which

Moses had revealed the irresistible power of the One God to those who worshipped the white bull, seemed to sanctify all the toil, and reward the weariness and pain which the quest after this "holy grail" of his enjoined.

On the 1st of April, Livingstone first sighted Lake Tanganika, at its southern extremity. The journey northward had been difficult. Here across a country suffering from tribal wars, and there among a people whose crops had failed, and where food was almost unobtainable. And yet, elsewhere, he would find a rich and prolific district, and the people well nourished. On his march, however, two men whom he had trusted implicitly deserted and carried off his medicine chest, with all the precious quinine and other remedies he possessed. This was indeed a loss of the first magnitude. Without medicine the European in Africa is almost helpless; henceforward he was to sustain attack after attack of fever and dysentery, in utter helplessness to ward them off or treat them properly. He says in his journal at the time, "I felt as if I had now received the sentence of death."

Though greatly impressed with the beauty and richness of the environment into which this southern tongue of the Tanganika had thrust itself, Livingstone was too ill to really enjoy the success he had gained. The absence of medicine brought on severe attacks of fever, and he had fits of insensibility which lasted for many hours at a time. For several days he lost all power in his lower limbs, and with the greatest difficulty entered a few notes into his journal.

On recovering strength enough to go forward, he passed along the western coast of the Lake for a short distance, and then struck westward in search of the lakes he had heard of in that region.

At the village of Ponda he fell in with a half-caste Arab who of late years has come in for a considerable

share of attention. This was none other than Tippo
Tippo, or Tippu Tip (which means "the-gatherer-
together-of-wealth"), whose Arab name is Hamid bin
Mohamed. Some eight years afterwards, Stanley
met him, and, much impressed by his ability, engaged his assistance for the first stages of the
descent of the Congo. It will be within the recol-
lection of most that when Stanley ascended the
Aruwhimi to plunge into the unknown region between
him and Emin Pasha, he appointed Tippu Tip Governor
of Stanley Falls. This act has occasioned some sur-
prise among many who are familiar with Tippu and
such men as he; but Stanley is a man of such capacity
that we may well wait before passing sentence on his
judgment.

Towards the end of November 1867, Livingstone
reached the town of the then Casembe or chief of the
Lunda tribes living between Lakes Moero and Bangweolo. On the 8th of that month he had discovered
Lake Moero, a lake of considerable extent, and girt
about with dense tropical vegetation. As the year
closed, he was again prostrated with a severe attack,
and in his journal we find the following entry for the
1st of January, 1868: "Almighty Father, forgive the sins
of the past year for Thy Son's sake. Help me to be
more profitable during this year. If I am to die this
year, prepare me for it."

The first six months of the year were occupied in
wanderings about the country which he had reached,
and on the 28th of July, 1868, he discovered Bangweolo,
one of the largest of the lakes of Central Africa. The
length of the lake is about a hundred and fifty miles, its
breadth seventy-five—or, in other words, it is somewhat
larger than Wales. Its shores differ from Moero, for
nearly all round are vast stretches of that "sponge" land
which has been previously described. In the course of
a march some thirty miles in length Livingstone crossed

no fewer than twenty-nine of these "sponges." The constant wettings, the continual wadings, the entire absence of medicinal remedies, soon told upon a weakened frame. His ability to travel became less as the attacks were more frequent, and the new year 1869 came in when Livingstone was lying on a bed of sickness and almost mortal pain.

He determined to go to Ujiji; and in company with a friendly Arab, by name Mohamed Bogharib, he set out for this important town on the eastern shores of Tanganika. The year previous to this step had been spent in investigating the sources of the river which he believed would prove to be the Nile—that river whose gift to the world is Egypt. That he was wrong we know now; but the indomitable pluck and tenacity with which he fought against every form of difficulty remains as a brilliant example of that genius which has been defined as the capacity for taking infinite pains.

When half-way to the Tanganika he became so ill that for the first time in the course of nearly thirty years he was carried when on the march. With the body, the mind seemed to be failing. In the trees as he passed along he saw figures and faces of men—even himself lying dead. "When I think of my children and friends," he says, "the lines ring through my head perpetually:

> 'I shall look into your faces
> And listen to what you say,
> And be often very near you
> When you think I'm far away.'"

On arriving at the lake, and after some delay, he was put into a canoe. "Patience," he says, "was never more needed than now. I am near Ujiji; but the slaves who paddle are tired, and no wonder; they keep up a roaring song all through their work night and day. . . . Hope to hold out to Ujiji."

On the 14th of March, the little party passed the mouth of the Malagarazi River, and the same day arrived at Ujiji.

CROSSING A "SPONGE."

CHAPTER X.

THE LAST JOURNEY.

AS soon as he had recovered sufficient strength to walk, Livingstone prepared to set out for Manyuema, which lay westward of the northern end of the lake, and for the Lualaba, which lay westward again of Manyuema. He started on the 12th of July, 1869, and reached Bambarré, a town in Manyuema, on the 21st of September.

The country of Manyuema was at that time quite unknown. Rumour, however, had given it a bad character. The people were reported to be cannibals; gorillas or sokos abounded in their country; and, although the richness of the region and density of its population were alike indisputable, terrible tales of peril were told by those who had pierced the interior. But Livingstone wished to ascertain the course of the Lualaba as it flowed northward, and if possible identify it with the Nile. No "travellers' tales" could deter him; so he started directly he could. He found in this country that every prospect was pleasing, and "only man was vile." The people were far too much addicted to the delights of palm-toddy, and the enervating effect of self-indulgence was already making this numerous race only too ripe for the raids of the Arabs and their slave-trading bands.

He made an attempt to navigate the Lualaba for some distance, but ill-health and the sullen obstinacy of the natives sent him back to Bambarré. In June 1870 he started again, accompanied only by three "faithfuls"—Susi, Chuma, and Gardner; but again failing health drove him back. For nearly three months he was laid up with ulcers on the feet, and this may help to explain the following remark in his journal: "I read the whole Bible through four times whilst I was in Manyuema."

But in spite of every difficulty he had done some geographical work, and had named some of the discoveries made. The river that issued from the chain of lakes which had been the scene of his many wanderings was called Webb's Lualaba, after his hospitable friend of Newstead Abbey; and its western branch became Young's Lualaba, after James Young. The latter stream issued from Lake Lincoln—named in honour of the emancipator of four million slaves in the United States. But while he was thus remembering old friends, and perhaps because of it, he became anxious to stay his steps for a long, long rest: "I have an intense and sore longing to finish and retire, and trust that the Almighty may permit me to go home." Yet elsewhere he says, with sublime resignation, "I commit myself to the Almighty Disposer of events."

The 1st of January, 1871, still finds him weak and waiting at Bambarré. Then ten men out of a much larger number arrived, sent from Zanzibar by Dr. Kirk, the consul, and Livingstone's old friend. They left Zanzibar with over forty letters for the Doctor: they arrived with one! They were worthless scoundrels, and slaves, to boot. As soon as he started westward with them they mutinied, and threatened to return to their comrades, whom they had left at Ujiji with the stores for the Doctor, and who were meanwhile living on them. By dint of great persistence, however, Livingstone managed to reach the Lualaba by the end of March, and to his deep disappointment he then found that the river had a somewhat westerly course, and was more probably the Congo than the Nile.

On reaching Nyangwé, his farthest point, he had an acute illustration of the horrors of slaving. During his stay in that settlement some Arabs massacred several hundreds of the inhabitants, without an hour's notice, in an attempt to establish their own power. From Nyangwé the carnage spread outwards, and village after village was soon in flames, and murder and robbery rampant. Moved to the depths of his heart, but unable to do anything to help the Manyuema, Livingstone attempted to renew his explorations; but, forced back by the worthless slaves who formed his escort, and who said that their masters at Zanzibar had told them to return on meeting him, he was compelled to retrace his steps to Ujiji, some six hundred miles distant. In the worst of health, a mere "ruckle of bones," as he put it, he arrived at Ujiji on the 23rd of October, only to find that the rascal who had charge of his stores had stolen the whole and converted them to his own use.

His body racked by pain and disease, his mind tormented by a series of bitter disappointments, his efforts thwarted and hopes blasted by the conduct of his very servants, and then on returning at last to Ujiji only to find that the means he required to buy even his daily bread had been dissipated by a scoundrel who had added to the crime of theft the vice of hypocrisy

LIVINGSTONE'S LAST JOURNEY.

(the fellow had divined on the Koran, and found that the Doctor was dead),—surely at this hour Livingstone was passing through a trial fiery enough to have consumed all his patience and resignation! But just at this moment, when his spirits were at their lowest ebb, help of the most unexpected kind was at hand.

On the 10th of November, 1871, a well-equipped caravan entered Ujiji to the usual accompaniment of gun-firing, shouting, and singing. Tents, saddles, kettles, and a large bath figured prominently on the heads of the *pagazis* or carriers. In front of the advancing company the American flag was carried, proclaiming to Livingstone the nationality of the new arrival. The caravan was that which was fitted out by Mr. Gordon Bennett, of the *New York Herald*, and the white man in command, who came forward with such emotion to grasp the Doctor's hands, was Henry M. Stanley, Welsh by birth and American by adoption, and the travelling correspondent of that enterprising paper. He came with unlimited resources at his back, not only to find Livingstone, but relieve him as well.

Owing to a native war which had closed the ordinary caravan route, Stanley had been obliged to leave most of his stores at Unyanyembe, the great Arab settlement between Ujiji and the east coast, and reach the lake by a circuitous path. It was arranged therefore that he and Livingstone should return together to Unyanyembe, and that the Doctor, who in spite of his many sufferings was determined not to go home till he had finished his work, should there receive a sufficient quantity of cloth, beads, and stores for his further explorations. While waiting at Ujiji, however, Stanley and he proceeded to the north end of the lake to ascertain, once and for all, if the river Lusizi drained the Tanganika or merely flowed into it. The latter was found to be the case and the long-disputed question of the connection of the Tanganika with the Victoria Nyanza or the Albert Nyanza was decided in the negative.

On returning from this discovery, Mr. Stanley was prostrated by fever; and, indeed, throughout the journey to Unyanyembe, which had been postponed for some weeks on account of his illness, he suffered more or less from fever, and at times was so weak that he had to be carried on the march. When Unyanyembe was reached—on the 18th of February, 1872—Stanley handed over to the Doctor a large amount of stores of every description, together with some goods which had been sent to Livingstone from England. The latter included four flannel shirts from his daughter Agnes, and two pairs of good English boots from Horace Waller. These presents were particularly welcome, as the Doctor had patched and cobbled his clothes till they would hardly hold together. Stanley then hurried to the coast, in order to send back a number of trusty men as carriers for the Doctor's goods. Moreover, he bore the precious journal, which dated from six years back, and contained a wealth of information about countries and peoples hitherto unexplored and unknown.

At Bagamoyo, the caravan port on the east coast, Stanley met the Geographical Society's Livingstone Relief Expedition. But their work had been anticipated; and, supposing that they could do nothing for the Doctor that had not been done, the officers in charge gave up the idea of going further, and returned to Europe.

When Livingstone shook Stanley's hand for the last time, he was parting with the only white man he had seen in the last six years, and the last he would see on this earth. The farewell between these two men was of a most affecting nature, for both knew of the difficulties of the past and the future; and during the four months in which they had lived together in no common degree of familiarity, they had regarded each other with the greatest interest: the one, a veteran who had borne the burden and heat of the day; the other, a young knight who had but just won his golden spurs. Although as unlike as possible in character, Stanley was to take up much of the work which the Doctor left unfinished, and carry it to a successful end. Moreover, he was to fill in the public eye as large if not so well-rounded a space; for although Stanley has little of the missionary about him, he has achieved such herculean labours in Africa, and has met with such unqualified success, that he may well be regarded as the greatest traveller since Livingstone's time.

In the meanwhile Livingstone was waiting at Unyanyembe for the men Stanley was to send. He employed much of the time in writing letters and noting down what he could learn from the Arabs. A few days after his parting with Stanley his fifty-ninth birthday occurred, and in his journal we find these words: "I again dedicate my whole self to Thee. Accept me, and grant, O gracious Father, that ere this year is gone I may finish my task. In Jesus' name I ask it. Amen; so let it be. David Livingstone."

In May he wrote a letter for the *New York Herald*, and it is in this letter that we find those words which have struck every reader with their pathetic intenseness, and which may now be seen inscribed upon his tomb in Westminster Abbey. Thus they run: "All I can add in my loneliness is, may Heaven's rich blessing come down on every one—American, English, or Turk —who will help to heal the open sore of the world." He was thinking, as ever, of the gaping wound which slavery had made.

Early in July he heard of Sir Roderick Murchison's death, and it touched him deeply that his old friend should not have lived to know of Stanley's success.

Murchison's constant support, through thick and thin, had always been a great source of comfort to the Doctor; and, speaking of the "sad intelligence," he says, "Alas! alas! this is the only time in my life I ever felt inclined to use the word, and it bespeaks a sore heart."

Later in the month, when reflecting in his journal on missions and the necessity for liberality of mind and charity, he says: "I have avoided giving offence to intelligent Arabs—who having pressed me, asking if I believed in Mohammed—by saying, 'No, I do not: I am a child of Jesus bin Miriam,' avoiding anything offensive in my tone."

At last the men whom Stanley had sent off arrived, and they proved to be a very good lot. Some had been with Stanley when he relieved Livingstone, and others were recruited from the Geographical Society's Expedition. The Doctor started almost immediately—on the 25th of August—and reached the Tanganika about six weeks later. Following the eastern shores, he rounded the southern point of the lake, and in bad health struck south, and then west for Lake Bangweolo.

The rainy season was upon them. Day after day it rained or drizzled or hailed, and the country rapidly underwent a change for the worst. Streams became rivers, and rivers mighty and resistless torrents. As the mountain slopes of Urungu were left behind, that disagreeable feature of African geography to which Livingstone introduced us—the "sponge"—became frequent. Where *terra firma* was met with, too often it was overlaid with knee-deep water. To make matters worse, the natives assumed an unfriendly attitude, and it became almost impossible to obtain food. Fever and an aggravated form of dysentery laid hold of the Doctor's worn-out body, and reduced his strength to such an extent that once again he had to be carried by his men on a *kitanda*, a light palanquin with a wooden framework. They were splashing through the endless sponges round the east end of Lake Bangweolo, and pushing forward through innumerable difficulties. All the symptoms of his illness became more acute, and he suffered most excruciating pain. Several times he fainted from loss of blood, and a drowsiness seemed to steal over him ever and again. The entries in his journal became shorter and shorter, until at last only the dates appeared: he was too weak to write more. Yet we learn from Susi and Chuma, his faithful servants, that he frequently asked questions of the natives with regard to distant hills, the rivers they were crossing, whence they came and whither they flowed.

On the 27th of April, 1873, his last entry is made in the journal. It must have cost a great effort, for all day he had lain in a stupor, brought on by intense weakness. These are the last words that he wrote:—

"27th April, 1873. Knocked up quite, and remain —recover—sent to buy milch goats. We are on the banks of the Molilamo."

To the last he preserved his habit of faithfully recording the geographical features of his position.

On the following day he was gently lifted off his bed, laid in a canoe, and ferried across the river. He was then as gently replaced on the *kitanda*, and borne along. He was now near the village of Chitambo, at the southern extremity of Bangweolo, and the men hastened to reach this resting-place. Through dreary stretches of water they steadily splashed their way. Whenever a fairly dry patch was reached, he begged them to lay him down and let him stay. The brave fellows did what they could to encourage him, and on the evening of the 29th they reached the village. During the day he had been so faint as to be unable to articulate at times. Some of the men had been thoughtfully sent on

LIVINGSTONE FOUND DEAD IN THE HUT

in front to build a hut for him, and shortly after arriving the Doctor was laid down upon his bed.

On the following morning the chief, Chitambo, came to call upon him, but the Doctor was too ill to talk with him. In the afternoon Susi placed his watch in the palm of the Doctor's hand, and held it there while for the last time the key was slowly and with difficulty turned. Some hours later, shortly before midnight, he asked Susi, "Is this the Luapula?" His mind was evidently failing.

An hour later, he asked Susi to bring the medicine chest. Selecting the calomel with great difficulty, he told Susi to pour some water into a cup, and then said in a low indistinct voice,—

"All right: you can go out now."

They were the last words that his fellow-creatures ever heard him speak.

Shortly before dawn on the 1st of May, a lad who slept within the hut to attend to his needs awoke Susi, Chuma, and two or three more, saying he feared the master was dead. They entered the hut, and by the dim light of the candle which was still burning they saw the Doctor kneeling on his knees beside the bed, his face resting on both hands, and his body leaning against the edge. They gazed in doubt for a few moments; but there was no stir, no breathing. One stepped forward and laid his hand on the worn and hollow cheek. It was cold. The master was indeed dead!

While in the act of praying to his God, the heroic soul had passed away. We shall never know what prayer he made; but, knowing the set purpose of his life, the great desire with which his whole being was possessed, we may well and with reverence think that in committing his spirit into the hands of the God who gave it he did not omit to plead for the healing of that great "open sore of the world," in probing which he had laid down his life.

One thing, however, was certain. The spirit of him who had travelled up and down Africa for over thirty years, whose heart was given to her cause, and whose feet never seemed to weary for her sake—this noble, glorious soul had now journeyed to that undiscovered country from whose bourn no traveller returns. Livingstone was dead. How much that meant! This "child of Jesus bin Miriam," this intensely human devotee to God, had laid down the cross only to receive the crown; he

"Climbed the steep ascent of heaven,
Through peril, toil, and pain;"

racked with bodily torment, he knelt beside his bed in far-away Ilala, and slept only to awake with Christ and be satisfied. "Africa, his own dear Africa, with all her woes and sins and wrongs," was to hear no more the voice of him crying in her wilderness; no more could he plead her cause before the great ones of the world. And yet, though the Light of that Dark Continent was itself darkened, the gleam would linger and illumine the gloomy places. Men would come and gaze, and kindle their torches as they followed in those well-known steps and fought afresh his old crusade, and little by little the light would steal over the mountains and ray down upon the rivers and lakes, and the people would turn toward it and say, "Behold, the Dayspring is at hand." And he who bore the torch through the long dark night will be remembered then. Not that he will need it—the toil and pain and sorrow will have vanished, and for ever. Ay, "Blessed are the dead that die in the Lord; for they rest from their labours, and their works do follow them."

The beauty of his character was not lost on the poor blacks who were with him. With a fidelity which is rare in story, and a sense of responsibility almost unknown in benighted Africa, his servants prepared to convey his body and personal effects back to his own people. They buried his heart and internal organs under a tree, and marked the grave so that it might be recognised. His body they dried in the sun, and embalmed in the best way they could. Wrapping it in calico and bark, and covering the whole with canvas, they set out on their long and difficult journey to Zanzibar. Numerous dangers threatened them, and time and again they were surrounded by hostile bands—hostile chiefly through a superstitious fear of the dead. But still they persevered; and, after behaving with a courage and devotion worthy of their beloved master, they at length brought his mortal remains safely to the coast, together with the whole of his personal effects. Nearly a year had been occupied by the journey. Not a note or jotting of all those last seven years of Livingstone's life was lost, and it is entirely owing to Susi and Chuma and their faithful companions that this is so. Our debt to these fine fellows no reward could wipe out. It is an enduring obligation.

On the 15th of April, 1874, the body, accompanied by Susi and Chuma, arrived in England. It was taken to the rooms of the Geographical Society, and there identified—partly by the false joint in the upper arm, which had developed when the lion mangled him long years before at Mabotsa.

Three days later, among those who had worked with him and for him, in the presence of the mighty dead as well as the mighty living, he was laid to rest in Westminster Abbey. Moffat and Oswell, Steele and Webb, Waller and Kirk, Young and Stanley, were there to pay a last tribute of affection to their old comrade; and all who were present were closely drawn to him through ties of admiration for his character and sympathy for his cause. In former years, when he returned from Africa, he had received the ringing

LIVINGSTONE'S FOLLOWERS BRINGING HIS BODY TO THE COAST.

welcome of a nation. Upon that day when he came again for the last time, as he was laid to rest in the Abbey, that nation, stricken with grief though hardly yet aware of all his greatness, bade him a mute farewell.

THE UNIVERSITIES MISSION STEAMER, "CHARLES JANSEN,' OFF LIVINGSTONIA

CHAPTER XI.

LIVINGSTONE'S LEGACY.

"WHEREVER," writes Professor Drummond, in his admirable book on "Tropical Africa"— a book which is distinguished by the merit of brevity among a score and more works on Africa as cumbrous as the subject with which they deal—" Wherever David Livingstone's footsteps are crossed in Africa, the fragrance of his memory seems to remain." Confirmation of this statement, though it is really unnecessary, is found in the following anecdote, told by the Rev. Chauncy Maples :—

"While staying with Matola, I was told there was a man who specially wanted to see his English visitors, because he had known something of a white man in old days, and if we were at all like him he should like to make our acquaintance. I desired that he might be presented to us. Forthwith he came—a pompous old man, who spoke in a dignified manner, and who had evidently some information to communicate. Over his right shoulder there hung an old coat—mouldy, partially eaten away, but still to be recognised as of decidedly English make and material. 'Whose was it?' I thought, as he began with much mystery to tell of a white man who, ten years ago, had travelled with him to Mataka's town; a white man, he said, whom to have once seen and talked with was to remember for ever; a white man who treated black men as his brothers, and whose memory would be cherished all along that Rovuma valley after we were all dead and gone. Then he described him—a short man with a bushy moustache and a keen, piercing eye, whose words were always gentle, and whose manners were always kind, whom as a leader it was a privilege to follow, and who knew the way to the hearts of all men. This was the description this African savage (as men speak) gave of Dr. Livingstone."

Livingstone's personality, indeed, has achieved more than even lasting impressions. He left the nation a rich legacy. He laid it upon their sense of right to carry on the work which had dropped from his hands. To this responsibility they have shown themselves awake, and the death of the most admirable labourer in the vast field of Africa gave an impetus to geographical and missionary enterprise, which has gone on increasing to the present time. By deeds, not words, we recall David Livingstone to mind; by deeds, not words, we expect to recognise his successors.

Livingstone's legacy is duplex in form. The first thing he left his countrymen to do was the extension of missionary teaching, coupled with the further development of those regions of Africa he had done so much to open to the Christian preacher. The second part of this legacy is a herculean task: it is nothing less than the eradication of slavery, chiefly by the substitution of legitimate commerce, and the fighting a crusade against those influences which foster the slave trade.

A brief history of how the first portion of this

bequest has been interpreted it is the province of this chapter to relate.

Almost the first sign of what has been called Livingstone's legacy is found in the search expedition of Mr. Edward Young, when the Doctor was yet living. Musa's lying story had reached England, and the Government despatched Mr. Young to ascertain whether the reported death of Livingstone were true. As has been related in this book, within the short space of eight months Mr. Young ascended the Zambesi and Shiré, and, by personal investigations on the southern shores of Lake Nyassa, proved the report to be without foundation. The question naturally arises, How was such speed possible, seeing that the steamer had to be taken to pieces, conveyed past the Murchison Cataracts, and put together again, going and coming? The answer is instructive. It was the name of Livingstone—the charm of that man's influence on the native mind—which enabled this to be done. Willing workers came in by hundreds, who not only laboured with eagerness at the task, but hailed the return of the English with unbounded joy. Mr. Young's passage up the Shiré was a triumphal progress. And this reception at the hands of the natives was not merely the exuberance of excitement, for there was proof to the contrary. The graves of those who died in the first days of the Universities Mission *had been kept scrupulously clean.* These were the firstfruits!

The next were posthumous. Two years after the Doctor's death, Mr. Young again ascended the Shiré, to again receive the welcome of the natives. The steamer which he brought with him upon this occasion was not to return. Livingstone's long-cherished aim was to be fulfilled. A steamer was to be placed on the waters of the Nyassa! His work was indeed being taken up, and in his own spirit too. For this was not the action of any one sect, but the united effort of all the Christian Churches of his native Scotland. The origin of this new mission was closely connected with Livingstone, for it was chiefly owing to Dr. James Stewart that the initiation of the enterprise took place; and long years before, at the time of Mrs. Livingstone's death, Dr. Stewart had come out to the Zambesi to see what could be done. He it was who laid the Doctor's beloved " Mary Moffat " to rest under the baobab tree at Shupanga, and spoke the words of consolation beside her grave. He had returned to Scotland, and reported that it would be better to wait a while; but, at the same time, he was deeply impressed with the harvest-field of which he had seen but a glimpse. He now stirred up the Churches; and, having fitted himself for more valuable work by entering the medical profession, he it was who renewed the work of Christ upon the shores of Nyassa.

This work has prospered greatly. Several of the missionaries are doctors, and are healing the bodies of those whose souls they are bringing to the Great Physician. At one place on the lake, at Bandawe, more than ten thousand visits have been registered in one year. Among the Angoni—those fierce marauding tribes for fear of whom Musa and his wretched Johanna comrades had deserted Livingstone—these medical officers are doing a great work. At Livingstonia, the chief settlement, which is situated on Cape Maclear, at Bandawe, and other stations, thousands and thousands of children have been taught to read and write the " sound words " of the Gospel of brotherly love. The writings of the Evangelists, the best hymns of the Churches, and works of smaller interest but great value, have been translated into the native tongue, so that the people may read and understand. And, further, still working in the spirit of Livingstone, the natives have been trained to preach to their fellows.

That they can be thus trained we have lately received

a striking testimony from Professor Drummond. Among his escort in Africa was one Moolu, a native Christian, whom he had taken from the mission station under Dr. Laws at Bandawe. "'Mission-blacks,'" he says, "in Natal and at the Cape are a by-word among the unsympathetic; but I never saw Moolu do an inconsistent thing. He could neither read nor write; he knew only some dozen words of English; until seven years ago he had never seen a white man; but I could trust him with everything I had. He was not 'pious;' he was neither bright nor clever; he was a commonplace black; but he did his duty, and never told a lie. The first night of our camp, after all had gone to rest, I remember being roused by a low talking. I looked out of my tent; a flood of moonlight lit up the forest; and there, kneeling upon the ground, was a little group of natives, and Moolu in the centre conducting evening prayers. Every night afterwards this service was repeated, no matter how long the march was nor how tired the men. I make no comment. But this I will say—Moolu's life gave him the right to do it."

Before reaching the lake, and half-way between Chibisa and Magomero, the first stations of the Universities Mission of 1862-64, there stand in the healthy district of the Shiré highlands the stations of Blantyre and Mandala. The idea of Blantyre is also Livingstone's, for it combines the industrial and the evangelical. It was started in 1876, the director being a medical missionary, and his five assistants artisans. From time to time this little force has been recruited, but the dominant idea has been maintained. To-day, if one visits the stations of Blantyre and Mandala, the good work achieved by the Church of Scotland is pleasantly visible. Many of the native lads who have been educated in the mission schools make admirable servants or interpreters for the active missionaries and their occasional guest, the African traveller; and the influence for peace and industry which these lonely lodges in the wilderness exert on the neighbouring tribes is remarkable. At Blantyre alone over £30,000 has been expended; and, fortunately, with excellent results. The buildings of the mission are of brick, and the land has been extensively cultivated. With the aid of skilled carpenters and gardeners a large industry has been developed, and private enterprise, conducted on sound lines, has helped to extend the efforts of the missionaries. Many of the sons of neighbouring chiefs have been and still are educated in the schools, and here and there are outposts officered by trained native teachers.

Passing northward and still in Livingstone's footsteps, we meet with the Universities Mission. Since 1877 this mission has been working on the mainland as well as at Zanzibar. Its sphere of labour has spread from the east coast to the shores of Nyassa itself. It has pushed on through Makuas and Yaos and Manganja, and placed its own steamer on the lake. Great difficulties have attended the opening up of this work, owing to the marauding Makwangwara, who devastate the cultivated fields of the more agricultural tribes, and render life uncertain and successful labour precarious. Enormous sums have been spent in developing this enterprise, and not without returns; but this would seem to be the most gigantic task which any of the societies have tackled, and progress must be estimated at a higher value. The unhealthy climate is not the least of the difficulties, and the mortality among the missionaries has been very great. Nearly a hundred agents are spread about this region, and they are constantly recruited from the headquarters at Zanzibar, where preachers, teachers, mechanics, and artisans are trained for the work. Considerably over £50,000 has been spent in this district; and, though costly both in lives and money, the influence of the disinterested conduct of the members of the mission has not been lost on the natives.

The Tanganika has been occupied by the London Missionary Society, which under the most hostile circumstances has done good work. Along the caravan route through Unyamwezi and Usagara, the Church Missionary Society has established stations, as well as devoting much of its strength to Uganda, the Victoria Nyanza, and the region between that lake and Mombasa. Many have fallen before the climate, some have perished by the sword, but the light of Gospel teaching and the beauty of dwelling together in unity have been made manifest.

Turning from this point on the east coast to far Angola on the west, the American Episcopalians are found hard at work. In neighbouring Benguela other American societies are labouring, and on the Congo the emissaries of the Baptist Society have achieved great things, geographical as well as missionary. The Livingstone Congo Mission is now in the hands of the American Baptists, but the work goes on. A circle of Christianity has been drawn round the dark region of Central Africa, and from north, south, east, and west radii of noble effort have pierced to the very heart.

And then the work of the pioneers—the achievements of those explorers who have followed in Livingstone's path, and made stable missionary effort possible—how great have these been!

They began with Stanley, who in 1874 landed in Africa to clear up once and for all the doubts which Livingstone and his co-workers north of the equator had left unsatisfied. The story of his circumnavigation of the Tanganika and Victoria Nyanza, of his exploration of Uganda, and the loyal service to Christianity which he did by persuading M'tesa to accept a Christian mission; his march through Karagwe to Nyangwe, how he took up the thread of discovery where

Livingstone had dropped it; his marvellous descent of the Lualaba, which he proved to be not the Nile nor the Niger, but the Congo,—are not these almost fabulous achievements, and the environment of peril and horror in which they are set, known to the world? In crossing Africa from the east coast to the west, and thereby, with Cameron, reversing the order of the first great trans-continental journey of Livingstone, Stanley put at rest a controversy which had raged with terrible warmth and for many years in scientific circles. He not only proved that the river which ran through Livingstone's chain of lakes in the very heart of the continent was *not* the Nile, but he found the head-waters of the Nile itself. But he did more than this; for he proved that for a thousand miles the Congo flowed without cataract or fall; for a thousand miles it was fitted to be a natural highway, from within a short distance of the coast to the centre of Africa— a highway whose value is simply incalculable. In doing all this he yet was but beginning; for a few years later he was building up a mighty state on the banks and in the basin of this river, by exploration, by conciliation, by commerce. The full measure of good which the Congo Free State may perform for Africa none of us can tell at the present time; but it may safely be said that if the African is to be redeemed and his continent included in the orderly progress of the world, it will be done by such commercial kingdoms as the Free State, which introduce the benefits of industry and commerce while they foster and protect the spread of a Gospel proclaiming the dignity of labour and the value of life.

And after Stanley comes a long array of workers in the same field. Joseph Thomson, surveying Eastern Africa with the eye of the geologist, proving the Lukuga to be the drain of the Tanganika, and thereby clearing up a much vexed point, and passing through unharmed—perhaps because not harming—the terrible Masai. H. H. Johnston at work in the district of Kilimanjaro, exploring the fever-haunted lagoons of the Niger Delta, and winning friends for himself and the English nation by a demeanour at once eager and courteous. Frederick Stanley Arnot, who of all travellers has perhaps kept closest to the model of Livingstone, the great master of them all. He is the man who, depending on no society for protection or funds, has spent seven years in Africa, doing a great work. His first object has ever been to preach the glad tidings; to him the most impressive sight in Africa is the great field "white unto the harvest." He has crossed Africa. In Katanga he has laboured with conspicuous success; and he has but lately returned to his self-appointed mission-field, bearing presents from England to Chitambo in acknowledgment—too tardy, alas!—of kindness shown to Livingstone, and subsequently to his followers after that martyr's death in his village.

And so the roll runs on—Cameron, journeying across Africa from Zanzibar to Benguela, surveying *en route* those southern shores of Lake Tanganika so familiar to Livingstone in his last years, reaching Nyangwe, the Doctor's most northerly point, and thence turning back, when on the very threshold of the discovery of the Congo, to travel to the west coast by the slave-paths through Urua and Ulunda; O'Neill, making nearly a score of journeys from the Mozambique coast into the interior, discovering the Lakes Amaramba and Chiuta, reaching Blantyre by a direct overland route, and surveying with marvellous accuracy every mile of his wanderings; Last, gathering in an ethnological harvest from the countries of the Southern Masai, Nguru, and neighbouring regions, and, like O'Neill, recording his journeys with that accuracy which makes them the more valuable; Selous, who has made the basin of the Zambesi his special province, who has trodden in Livingstone's footsteps and pierced the unknown countries on either hand; Keith Johnston, most expert of geographers, who succumbed to the climate before he had been able to set an indelible mark upon the country; Hore, with his brave wife, creating at Kavala Island, in the Lake Tanganika, a base for operations among the populous tribes surrounding the lake, investigating native character and language, inquiring into the natural science of the region, acting as an interpreter for the commercial needs of the teeming millions, and proving to demonstration the comparative healthiness of the climate in that locality.

And the list is not exhausted yet. Without reckoning one of the many explorers of other nationalities, the names of the fellow-countrymen of Livingstone follow on one another without a break. Maples, Johnson, Stewart, Grenfell, Comber, Wakefield—as one drops out of the line another stepping forward to fill his place. Working a thousand miles apart or side by side, they are all working to but one issue; for "the end of the geographical feat is only the beginning of the missionary enterprise."

HEADQUARTERS OF THE AFRICAN LAKES COMPANY, MANDALA.

CHAPTER XII.

LIVINGSTONE'S LEGACY (*continued*).

THE other half of the legacy which Livingstone left to his country is the eradication of the slave trade. With it are coupled conditions which his knowledge and foresight led him to lay down—the abolition of slavery by the substitution of legitimate commerce, and determined contention with the influences which foster the traffic in slaves.

For a generation and more Central Africa has been under a reign of terror—the reign of the Arabs. The advance of the Arab in Africa has steadily spread in an ever-widening path from the starting-point of Zanzibar until it has covered, like a hideous leprous blotch, the whole of the equatorial regions. The advance has been slow, and until late years marked by caution. The Arab came among the ignorant hordes who dwelt in comparative peace, cultivating the fertile soil. He came with open hand, exchanged his calicoes and beads and wire for the ivory of the elephant, and generally paid his way.

Gradually, however, as his strength grew and he learnt more of the childish nature of the people he went amongst, his cunning suggested another policy. He mixed in native politics, stirred up one tribe against the other, and took their part in war. For this help he demanded payment—payment like Shylock, in his "pound of flesh." This he received. What did the easy-going natives want with their captives in war? They had no idea of employing labour on their fields—the fields themselves required no more than the wives of the owners gave. Stronger and stronger grew the invader. He thought no longer of paying his way, but marched boastfully through the country at the head of his armed ruffians, and burnt here, robbed there, and captured everywhere. The conquest was complete. The Arab reign of terror had arrived.

It was the beginning of this final stage which Livingstone witnessed at Nyangwe, when over three hundred wretched natives, men, women, and children, were shot down with wanton cruelty. He wrote home about this atrocity, and roused public opinion in no common degree. Investigations on the coast gave an inkling of what was proceeding in the interior. It was estimated that from the Arab port of Kilwa, alone, more than twenty thousand slaves were annually exported. But Livingstone had said that for every slave that arrived at the coast two had died or been slaughtered in the interior. The outcome of his efforts was that British men-of-war blockaded the east coast, and largely checked the export of slaves. And yet this was of scant avail; the mouth of the sewer was indeed closed, but the foul stream was only diverted, to overflow the land and circulate its fatal poison. The action of the slave trade oscillated to and fro, from east to west, and north to south. The greed of the natives was appealed to, and men sold the helpless or the young of their own tribe—relatives even sold each other. Habit is second nature, and custom led these wretched people to regard slavery as natural. With fearful loss of life, the population of one district was deported to another, and that again elsewhere, and so on *ad infinitum* as long as gain could be acquired.

The roots of the trade had now struck deep. The simple, almost patriarchal, life of the agricultural races ceased to exist. Like the swoop of the fish-eagle the Arab came down upon the scattered villages and burnt and captured, and the weak tribes lived in terror while the strong prepared for the trader by raiding among the weak. One village became suspicious of the other, and the dwellings of the people retreated more and more to the gloom of the forest or the islands of the lake. In some districts the evil was so accentuated that three natives could not be sent on a message " in case two should combine and sell the third before they returned !"

And the woe of it—the desolation ! A year or so ago the region around the south end of Tanganika teemed with life and simple industry. To-day the march of the Arab can be followed by the charred embers which mark the villages, and the skeletons by the roadside which are all that is left of the people. Wissman, when descending the Kasai and travelling among the Basonge, passed through enormous villages—or rather towns— six and seven miles in length, whose dense population cultivated the land for many miles around. A year or so after he came to the same places—the fields were sprouting jungles, the houses mere heaps of ash and tinder. When Livingstone and Stanley travelled through Manyuema nothing struck them more than the hordes of inhabitants. To-day Manyuema is a wilderness. From Nyangwe to Stanley Falls, Tippu Tip and men of his calibre have devastated vast tracts of country, and the whole region lying west and south of Lakes Moero and Bangweolo is depopulated. The

Kasai on the west and the hilly country of the Masai on the east, from the head waters of the Koango to the lower waters of the Rovuma, and from the Manganja, 15° south of the equator, to the Soudanese of Kordofan, 15° north of it, Africa is harassed by these fiends in human form.

The slave trade would seem to arouse and feed the worst passions. The most gratuitous villainy accompanies it, and by sheer wanton cruelty thousands of lives are sacrificed. About two years ago "the Arabs at the north end of Lake Nyassa, after destroying fourteen villages with many of their inhabitants, pursued the population of one village into a patch of tall dry grass, set it on fire, surrounded it, and slew with the bullet and the spear those who crawled out from the more merciful flames." This was done because the people had given them trouble or had tried to escape. Rather than give the wretched people a chance of life, the men and women who from utter weakness are unable to march with the gang are tied tightly to a wayside tree and left to die of starvation. If any slaves escape, the survivors are made to feel the anger of their captors. The Arabs think nothing of hacking to death some of the weaklings in their caravan. If a young mother is seen staggering under her load, her babe is torn from her and flung into the grass by the track, there to be devoured by the hyænas or pecked to death by the birds of prey.

The head of the Blantyre Mission, the Rev. D. C. Scott, is quoted to the following effect by Mr. James Stevenson, of the African Lakes Company, in his stirring little pamphlet on the subject of Arab villainy and Portuguese indifference:—

"The Arab slave trade is making frightful progress. Caravans of Arabs are pouring in—for trade? No! Hardly a bale of cloth goes up country from the east coast; it is guns and powder, not even spirits. It is simply slaughter, and slaughter of thousands, and the desolation of the fairest lands—lands where the natives were at peace, where industry and thrift and happiness ruled; where to get through one village you might start in the early morning and not pass out of it till the sun was half-way down, journeying straight on; and these are now desolate. Fresh routes are opening up to them, and the desolation is spreading. It is not slave trade; it is ruthless massacre of the most barbarous type."

"Ruthless massacre!" Well may the African in his anguish say—so often that it has become a proverb— "God made the whites and God made the blacks, but the devil made the Arabs."

What does Stanley—a cool, level-headed man, not likely to be led away by sentiment, and of unparalleled experience in Africa—say on the subject? This:—

"The slave traders admit they have only 2,300 captives in this fold, yet they have raided through the length and breadth of a country larger than Ireland, bringing fire and spreading carnage with lead and iron. Both banks of the river show that 118 villages and 43 districts have been devastated, out of which is only educed this scanty profit of 2,300 females and children and about 2,000 tusks of ivory. The spears, swords, bows, and the quivers of arrows show that many adults have fallen. Given that 118 villages were peopled only by 1,000 each, we have only a profit of 2 per cent., and by the time all these captives have been subjected to the accidents of the river voyage to Kirundu and Nyangwe, of camp life and its harsh miseries, to the havoc of small-pox, and the pests which miseries breed, there will only remain a scant 1 per cent. upon the bloody venture."

Cardinal Lavigerie, with his estimate of two million massacred for the four hundred thousand annually brought to the coast, was well within the mark. A single sentence from one of his speeches will reveal to us the fate of some of these two million: "When caught, the unmarketable ones are either killed or left to die of hunger; the women are usually violated and then burnt."

It would almost seem that Livingstone's idea of substituting legitimate commerce for the trade in slaves is now out of date and powerless to stem the flood. As regards isolated endeavours to attain this end, this may be so; but there can be no doubt that organized commerce, the creation of great commercial states, or the development of those which already exist, may hope with some assurance of success to combat the evil.

A good deal has been done on these lines. The Congo Free State has advanced civilization in no small degree within its sphere of influence. The savage tribes have been shown the benefits of peace and trade, and the advantages to be reaped from contact with the civilized world. Commerce has been made possible by the opening up of rivers and roads, by the founding of stations and cultivation of soil, by consistent conciliatory measures and the establishment of a general security. Above all, the natives dwelling within a large portion of the state have been protected from the horrors of the slave trade. The British East Africa Company are attempting to do something of the same kind between the east coast and the Victoria Nyanza, and the Germans are showing the world how not to do it between Zanzibar and Unyamwezi.

The pluckiest and perhaps the most successful effort to introduce commerce of a legitimate order into Africa has been made by the African Lakes Company. This is no mere commercial enterprise, for its prime object is philanthropic—to oust the slave trade in Nyassaland by the introduction of commerce. It started operations about ten years ago, and has gradually widened and lengthened its field ever since. With several steamers on Nyassa and the Shiré, and over a dozen trading stations along the route, the company has provided plenty of scope for native energy. But it has done more. The famous "Stevenson Road," from the head of Lake Nyassa to the southernmost point of the Tanganika, has been constructed entirely by natives under the engineering direction of the late Mr. James Stewart. The natives proved themselves very well able to work, keeping to regular labour hours, and handling their pick-axes, crowbars, and spades with something like European skill. A station has been erected on the road and one on the Tanganika, and the chain of communication from the sea completed. In addition to this, native produce is bought in large quantities, and the people are encouraged to keep on increasing the quantity. Many experiments have been made with seeds not indigenous to the country; and, in short, whatever common sense has suggested should be done has been done.

Subsidiary to this company, but actuated by its enlightened motives, are the extensive coffee and sugar plantations at Zomba, belonging to two brothers named Buchanan, which rival in extent and fertility those of the Moirs, the managers of the Lakes Company at Mandala. A large native population is already dependent on these industries. Before long, there can be little doubt that the coffee trade of the Shiré highlands will prove a highly remunerative as well as salutary industry. As a reward to these brave pioneers, and for the sake of the harassed native, it is to be hoped that such will prove to be the case.

The difficulty, however, remains: How can commerce be given a fair chance and the slave trade a set-back? Things have come to such a pass, that but one suggestion seems feasible. A powerful company, or agglomeration of companies, should be formed to control British commercial interests from the Shiré to the head of the Tanganika. Along the lakes its police steamers should ply, and on the elevated spurs and hills in this lake region bodies of well-drilled native police should be held in reserve for any contingency. The points where the caravan routes intersect this long north-and-south line of water communication should be regarded as points of resistance, and measures taken accordingly. The whole of the east coast should again be jealously watched by gunboats, and such coigns of vantage as Zanzibar, Kilwa, and the like, should, by treaty, be declared free ports in the sense that no slave should be known within their limits. Ivory "rings" and "corners" might well be created in order to deprive the Arab of a great source of profit, and so starve him out.

The chief influence against such a settlement, or, indeed, any settlement of the question as regards Nyassaland and its more immediate districts, is the Portuguese indifference to all enterprise; and, first and foremost, all English enterprise. Portugal has neither men, nor money, nor commercial genius to develop one-quarter of the country she claims; but she is not, on account of that, any more likely to tolerate the capping of the edifice which British perseverance has reared out of blank savagery. Portugal, in fact, has neither a great colonial policy nor a statesman with an altruistic idea. Her attitude on the Mozambique coast and the Zambesi has resembled that of a certain dog that once made himself disagreeable in a manger.

The Congo has been declared free, and there is no reason against—indeed, every reason for—the Zambesi being also opened to the commerce of the world. The peculiar circumstances which make up the history of Portuguese settlement upon the banks of this river prevent the substantiation, if they do not prevent the making, of the Portuguese claim for its appropriation. Moreover, the Zambesi is a highway, a natural highway, to regions exploited and occupied by the English, to vast countries which are being solely developed by English exertion and English expenditure. By the canons of that most impartial of tests—International Law—Portugal has no legal right to bar free access or commerce to those regions and peoples beyond her immediate province, even though that province lie in the direct track; and the consensus of the civilized world is in harmony with legal principle when it withholds the moral support of its approbation. The claim of supremacy which is made by the Portuguese rests historically on some decree of Pope Alexander VI. —that Borgia of the Borgias; but practically on her possession of Mozambique on the east coast and Angola on the west coast. The great breadth of Africa lying between these extremities is therefore usurped by Portugal—on paper. This point must not be overlooked; for in reality, and in spite of centuries of nominal control on both coasts, the Portuguese have never developed the resources of their own province, benefited or even influenced the natives of the district adjoining that province, nor colonized or in any way exploited the enormous zone of country beyond. For so shadowy a claim as this, that great commercial and political highway which runs from the Zambesi delta up the Shiré, throughout the length of Nyassa and thence, *viâ* the Stevenson Road, to Tanganika, and on from there, by porterage, to the Congo and its Free State, must not be sealed to international and legitimate commerce. To the many commercial and civilizing influences which are rapidly converging on the heart of Africa, and striving for the suppression of that slave trade which is its heart-disease, Portugal cannot be allowed to give their *quietus*.

It should be remembered that Britain claims "a fair field and no favour" for all nations, and not merely for herself; that this is her attitude in spite of the fact that she has been almost alone in developing these portions of Africa and fighting against the influence of the Arab slave trader.

Portugal was first on the Zambesi, that is true; but Livingstone showed most conclusively that she had never utilized her position by Christianizing the natives, or in any way opening up the country; and, indeed, that she was there on sufferance. She fostered the slave trade in those days by conniving at its indulgence; to-day she fosters it by holding back those who would suppress it. It was Livingstone who led the way from Loanda to Quilimane; Livingstone who first ascended the Shiré, discovered Lakes Shirwa and Nyassa, and planted the first steamers on the Zambesi. It was British money that made the roads past the Murchison Cataracts, and from Nyassa to Tanganika; that established regular communication from the Nyassa to the Indian Ocean. British energy and pluck have striven for thirty years against the forces of barbarism and the somnolence of an effete power; those were British lives which are laid in that long series of graves from the Zambesi to the Nyassa; and a British sense of justice demands that Portugal should give every facility to the chivalrous attack on the slave trade which, with fearful odds against them, a mere handful of noble-hearted Britons are making, mindful of that saintly hero who wrote down his life-long prayer, exactly a year before his death, in these words:—

"All I can add in my loneliness is, may Heaven's rich blessing come down on every one—American, English, or Turk—who will help to heal this open sore of the world!"

Printed by Hazell, Watson, & Viney, Ld., London and Aylesbury.

www.ingramcontent.com/pod-product-compliance
Lightning Source LLC
Chambersburg PA
CBHW030307170426
43202CB00009B/906